REXX AND WMI

Using WbemScripting and Get

Richard Thomas Edwards

CONTENTS

Getting Started
The Wbemscripting Primer

'm not going to waste time here, we have a lot to cover and I don't want to bore you with my ramblings.

The first thing you need to know about WbemScripting is why it was called Wbemscripting in the first place. The WBem part stands for Web Based Enterprise Management. The problem with it was – and still is – the concept was based on a Microsoft business model that says something over 7 years should be retired.

Well, if you go by my own awareness of the product, it should have been retired three times by now and it is still going strong and is growing in strength and power.

Bottom line, it is a beast!

But one you can handle because it is all based on Windows Management Instrumentation (WMI).

These are all optional and there is a rule which states when you are running this on the local machine you do not use UserName or Password.

Anyway, most of the examples you see on the web go like this:

```
locator = .OLEObject~new("WbemScripting.SWbemLocator")
svc = Locator~ConnectServer(".", "root\cimv2")
```

And that works perfectly fine, but if you really want the full power of the call:

```
locator = .OLEObject~new("WbemScripting.SWbemLocator")
svc = Locator~ConnectServer(".", "root\cimv2", "", "", "MS_409", "", 0 , Nothing)
```

And let's continue with this:

```
svc~Security_~AuthenticationLevel = 6 'PacketPrivacy
svc~Security_~ImpersonationLevel = 3 'Impersonate
svc~Security_~Privileges~Add()
svc~Security_~Privileges~Remove()
```

Our next step is to add the SWbemServices Get function:

```
ob = svc~Get("Win32_Process")
```

What get does for us is two things. It lets us peer under the hood of the class and know more about it and what its capabilities are. Nice to know, right?

Only problem is not all classes provide this information. Only the popular ones do.

With that said, the actual call to get this information is:

```
ob = svc~Get("Win32_Process", 131072)
```

But we really aren't interested in knowing what is going on under the hood, we want the information returned by the call and that happens with the next line of code:

```
objs = ob~Instances_(0)
```

Now, we're ready to process the information into something we can use.

One of two coding templates we will be using are below.

For Horizontal views:

```
crlf = '0D0A'x

locator = .OLEObject~new("WbemScripting.SWbemLocator")
svc = Locator~ConnectServer(".", "root\cimv2", "", "", "MS_409", "", 0 , Nothing)
svc~Security_~AuthenticationLevel = 6 'PacketPrivacy
```

```
svc~Security_~ImpersonationLevel = 3 'Impersonate
ob = svc~Get("Win32_Process")
objs = ob~Instances_(0)

Do obj over objs
   Do prop over obj~Properties_
      Value = GetValue(prop, obj~GetObjectText_)
      say prop~name || ": " || Value || crlf
   End
End

GetValue:

Parse Arg name, tempstr


   pname = prop~Name || " = "

   P  = Pos(pname, tempstr)
   if (P > 0) THEN Do
      P = P || Length(pname)
      tempstr = SubStr(tempstr, P, Length(tempstr))
      p  = Pos( ";", tempstr)
      tempstr = substr(tempstr, 1, P-1)
      tempstr = changestr("{", tempstr, "")
      tempstr = changestr("}", tempstr, "")
      tempstr = changestr('"', tempstr, "")
      tempstr~strip
      if Length(tempstr) > 13 THEN Do
         if prop~CIMType = 101 THEN do
            Value = SubStr(tempstr, 5, 2) || "/" || SubStr(tempstr, 7, 2) || "/" ||
SubStr(tempstr, 1, 4) || " " || SubStr(tempstr, 9, 2) || ":" || SubStr(tempstr, 11, 2) ||
":" || SubStr(tempstr, 13, 2)
```

```
                tempstr = Value
            End
          End
          return tempstr
        End
        ELSE Do
            return ""
        End
      EXIT


      :: requires "OREXXOLE.CLS"


      For Vertical views:


      crlf = '0D0A'x


      locator = .OLEObject~new("WbemScripting.SWbemLocator")
      svc = Locator~ConnectServer(".", "root\cimv2", "", "", "MS_409", "", 0 ,
Nothing)
      svc~Security_~AuthenticationLevel = 6 'PacketPrivacy
      svc~Security_~ImpersonationLevel = 3 'Impersonate
      ob = svc~Get("Win32_Process")
      objs = ob~Instances_(0)
      obj1 = objs~ItemIndex(0)
      Do prop over obj1~Properties_
         Do obj over objs
            Value = GetValue(prop, obj~GetObjectText_)
            say prop~name || ": " || Value || crlf
         End
      End


      GetValue:
```

```
Parse Arg name, tempstr

   pname = prop~Name || " = "

   P  = Pos(pname, tempstr)
   if (P > 0) THEN Do
      P = P || Length(pname)
      tempstr = SubStr(tempstr, P, Length(tempstr))
      p  = Pos( ";", tempstr)
      tempstr = substr(tempstr, 1, P-1)
      tempstr = changestr("{", tempstr, "")
      tempstr = changestr("}", tempstr, "")
      tempstr = changestr('"', tempstr, "")
      tempstr~strip
      if Length(tempstr) > 13 THEN Do
         if prop~CIMType = 101 THEN do
            Value = SubStr(tempstr, 5, 2) || "/" || SubStr(tempstr, 7, 2) || "/" ||
SubStr(tempstr, 1, 4) || " " || SubStr(tempstr, 9, 2) || ":" || SubStr(tempstr, 11, 2) ||
":" || SubStr(tempstr, 13, 2)
            tempstr = Value
         End
      End
      return tempstr
   End
   ELSE Do
      return ""
   End
EXIT
```

:: requires "OREXXOLE.CLS"

As you can see from these two examples, the only real differences in them is the way they use the information that is being generated by the request. This one for horizontal:

```
Do obj over objs
   Do prop over obj~Properties_
      Value = GetValue(prop, obj~GetObjectText_)
      say prop~name || ": " || Value || crlf
   End
End
```

And this one for vertical:

```
obj1 = objs~ItemIndex(0)
Do prop over obj1~Properties_
   Do obj over objs
      Value = GetValue(prop, obj~GetObjectText_)
      say prop~name || ": " || Value || crlf
   End
End
```

The rest of the code has been separated from the rather canned routines – I use them in each book – that I'm using for each book and yes, I know you don't want to pay money for the same routines over again, but you may only need the routines for a specific SWbemServices function and never buy another book again. I must count on this being the first and only time you will be purchasing one of these and make sure the routines you may want to use are available here for you cut and paste.

Example of Cutting and Pasting
Not as hard as you think

O k, so, you have seen the code to drive the output BLOWN HTML REPORT?

```
crlf = '0D0A'x

locator = .OLEObject~new("WbemScripting.SWbemLocator")
service = locator~connectServer(".", "root\cimv2")
ob = svc~Get("Win32_Process")
objs = ob~InstancesOf_(0)

WriteTheCode(objs)


WriteTheCode:
objs = ARG(1)

ws = .OLEObject~new("WScript.Shell")
tstr = ws~CurrentDirectory || "\Win32_Process.html"
fso = .OLEObject~new("Scripting.FileSystemObject")
txtstream = fso~OpenTextFile(tstr, 2, .true, -2)
```

```
txtstream~WriteLine("<html>")
txtstream~WriteLine("<head>")
txtstream~WriteLine("<style type='text/css'>")
txtstream~WriteLine("th")
txtstream~WriteLine("{")
txtstream~WriteLine("   COLOR: darkred;")
txtstream~WriteLine("   BACKGROUND-COLOR: white;")
txtstream~WriteLine("   FONT-FAMILY: Cambria, serif;")
txtstream~WriteLine("   FONT-SIZE: 12px;")
txtstream~WriteLine("   text-align: left;")
txtstream~WriteLine("   white-Space: nowrap;")
txtstream~WriteLine("}")
txtstream~WriteLine("td")
txtstream~WriteLine("{")
txtstream~WriteLine("   COLOR: navy;")
txtstream~WriteLine("   BACKGROUND-COLOR: white;")
txtstream~WriteLine("   FONT-FAMILY: Cambria, serif;")
txtstream~WriteLine("   FONT-SIZE: 12px;")
txtstream~WriteLine("   text-align: left;")
txtstream~WriteLine("   white-Space: nowrap;")
txtstream~WriteLine("}")
txtstream~WriteLine("</style>")
txtstream~WriteLine("<title>Win32_Process</title>")
txtstream~WriteLine("</head>")
txtstream~WriteLine("<body>")
txtstream~WriteLine("<table Border='0' cellpadding='1' cellspacing='1'>")
Do obj over objs
   txtstream~WriteLine("<tr>")
   Do prop over obj~Properties_
      txtstream~WriteLine("<th>" || prop~Name || "</th>")
   End
   txtstream~WriteLine("</tr>")
   LEAVE
```

```
End
Do obj over objs
  txtstream~WriteLine("<tr>")
  Do prop over obj~Properties_
    txtstream~WriteLine("<td>" || GetValue(prop~Name, obj) || "</td>")
  End
  txtstream~WriteLine("</tr>")
End
txtstream~WriteLine(</table>")
txtstream~WriteLine("</body>")
txtstream~WriteLine("</html>")
txtstream~close

Exit

GetValue:

name = ARG(1)
obj = ARG(2)

  tempstr = obj~GetObjectText_
  pname = name || " = "

  P  = Pos(pname, tempstr)
  if (P > 0) THEN Do
    P = P || Length(pname)
    tempstr = SubStr(tempstr, P, Length(tempstr))
    p  = Pos( ";", tempstr)
    tempstr = substr(tempstr, 1, P-1)
    tempstr = changestr("{", tempstr, "")
    tempstr = changestr("}", tempstr, "")
    tempstr = changestr('"', tempstr, "")
    tempstr~strip
```

```
if Length(tempstr) > 13 THEN Do
  if prop~CIMType = 101 THEN do
     Value = SubStr(tempstr, 5, 2) || "/" || SubStr(tempstr, 7, 2) || "/" ||
SubStr(tempstr, 1, 4) || " " || SubStr(tempstr, 9, 2) || ":" || SubStr(tempstr, 11, 2) ||
":" || SubStr(tempstr, 13, 2)
       tempstr = Value
    End
  End
  return tempstr
End
ELSE Do
  return ""
End

EXIT

:: requires "OREXXOLE.CLS"
```

Are you beginning to see why I continually mention that this book is a lot more code than what the pages are telling you? This single routine used 3 full pages.

The ASP routines take up 6 full pages (counting the half pages as one.

The example above, around 100 lines of code. Using the biggest stylesheet – the one that produced the table below – takes 249 lines of code:

Caption	CommandLine	CreationClassName	CreationDate	CSCreationClassName	CSName
System		Win32_Process		Win32_ComputerSyst	WIN-VN
System		Win32_Process	06/03/2018	Win32_ComputerSyst	WIN-VN
smss.e		Win32_Process	06/03/2018	Win32_ComputerSyst	WIN-VN
csrss.e		Win32_Process	06/03/2018	Win32_ComputerSyst	WIN-VN
wininit	wininit.exe	Win32_Process	06/03/2018	Win32_ComputerSyst	WIN-VN
csrss.e		Win32_Process	06/03/2018	Win32_ComputerSyst	WIN-VN
service		Win32_Process	06/03/2018	Win32_ComputerSyst	WIN-VN
lsass.e	C:\\Windows	Win32_Process	06/03/2018	Win32_ComputerSyst	WIN-VN

Working with ASP
The concept of programs writing programs

want to share something with you here that should help clear up an issue even the pros have issues with. When you use txtstream~WriteLine("") what is in between the quotes is considered a string until that string is being read by the program or script that needs to render it.

So, if I write: txtstream~WriteLine("<html>") there is no issue here because the code is pure html.

But if I write: txtstream~WriteLine("Response.Write(""<tr>""" & vbcrlf) "), what do you think is going to happen when VBScript tries to use:

Response.Write("<tr>" & vbcrlf)? It is going to produce a runtime error because it doesn't know what to do with the ||.

Just remember that what's inside those quotes is considered a string but once that string is rendered instructing the script or code what to do has to be native to the code running it. And, in this case, it needs to be written like this:

Response.Write("<tr>" & vbcrlf)

With that off my chest, below is the code for ASP

WriteTheCode:

```
objs = ARG(1)

ws = .OLEObject~new("WScript.Shell")
txtstream = fso~OpenTextFile(ws~CurrentDirectory || "\Win32_Process.asp",
2, true, -2)
```

For Single Line Horizontal

```
txtstream~WriteLine("<html>")
txtstream~WriteLine("<head>")
txtstream~WriteLine("<style type='text/css'>")
txtstream~WriteLine("th")
txtstream~WriteLine("{")
txtstream~WriteLine("   COLOR: darkred;")
txtstream~WriteLine("   BACKGROUND-COLOR: white;")
txtstream~WriteLine("   FONT-FAMILY: Cambria, serif;")
txtstream~WriteLine("   FONT-SIZE: 12px;")
txtstream~WriteLine("   text-align: left;")
txtstream~WriteLine("   white-Space: nowrap;")
txtstream~WriteLine("}")
txtstream~WriteLine("td")
txtstream~WriteLine("{")
txtstream~WriteLine("   COLOR: navy;")
txtstream~WriteLine("   BACKGROUND-COLOR: white;")
txtstream~WriteLine("   FONT-FAMILY: Cambria, serif;")
txtstream~WriteLine("   FONT-SIZE: 12px;")
txtstream~WriteLine("   text-align: left;")
txtstream~WriteLine("   white-Space: nowrap;")
txtstream~WriteLine("}")
txtstream~WriteLine("</style>")
txtstream~WriteLine("<title>Win32_Process</title>")
txtstream~WriteLine("</head>")
txtstream~WriteLine("<body>")
```

Use this if you want to create a border around your table:

txtstream~WriteLine("<table Border='1' cellpadding='1' cellspacing='1'>")

Use this if you don't want to create a border around your table:

txtstream~WriteLine("<table Border='0' cellpadding='1' cellspacing='1'>")

txtstream~WriteLine("<%")
obj = objs~ItemIndex(0)
txtstream~WriteLine("Response.Write(""<tr>"" & vbcrlf)")
for Each prop in obj~Properties_
    txtstream~WriteLine("Response.Write(""<th>" || prop~Name || "</th>"" & vbcrlf)")
next
txtstream~WriteLine("Response.Write(""</tr>"" & vbcrlf)")
txtstream~WriteLine("Response.Write(""<tr>"" & vbcrlf)")

for Each prop in obj~Properties_
    txtstream~WriteLine("Response.Write(""<td>" || GetValue(prop~Name, obj) || "</td>"" & vbcrlf)")
next
txtstream~WriteLine("Response.Write(""</tr>"" & vbcrlf)")
txtstream~WriteLine("%>")
txtstream~WriteLine(</table>")
txtstream~WriteLine("</body>")
txtstream~WriteLine("</html>")
txtstream~close

For Multi Line Horizontal

txtstream~WriteLine("<html>")
txtstream~WriteLine("<head>")
txtstream~WriteLine("<style type='text/css'>")

```
txtstream~WriteLine("th")
txtstream~WriteLine("{")
txtstream~WriteLine("    COLOR: darkred;")
txtstream~WriteLine("    BACKGROUND-COLOR: white;")
txtstream~WriteLine("    FONT-FAMILY: font-family: Cambria, serif;")
txtstream~WriteLine("    FONT-SIZE: 12px;")
txtstream~WriteLine("    text-align: left;")
txtstream~WriteLine("    white-Space: nowrap;")
txtstream~WriteLine("}")
txtstream~WriteLine("td")
txtstream~WriteLine("{")
txtstream~WriteLine("    COLOR: navy;")
txtstream~WriteLine("    BACKGROUND-COLOR: white;")
txtstream~WriteLine("    FONT-FAMILY: font-family: Cambria, serif;")
txtstream~WriteLine("    FONT-SIZE: 12px;")
txtstream~WriteLine("    text-align: left;")
txtstream~WriteLine("    white-Space: nowrap;")
txtstream~WriteLine("}")
txtstream~WriteLine("</style>")
txtstream~WriteLine("<title>Win32_Process</title>")
txtstream~WriteLine("</head>")
txtstream~WriteLine("<body>")
```

Use this if you want to create a border around your table:
```
txtstream~WriteLine("<table Border='1' cellpadding='1' cellspacing='1'>")
```

Use this if you don't want to create a border around your table:
```
txtstream~WriteLine("<table Border='0' cellpadding='1' cellspacing='1'>")
```

```
txtstream~WriteLine("<%")
obj = objs~ItemIndex(0)
txtstream~WriteLine("Response.Write(""<tr>"" & vbcrlf)")
for Each prop in obj~Properties_
```

```
            txtstream~WriteLine("Response.Write(""<th>" || prop~Name || "</th>""" &
vbcrlf)")
        next
        txtstream~WriteLine("Response.Write(""</tr>""" & vbcrlf)")
        For Each obj in objs
            txtstream~WriteLine("Response.Write(""<tr>""" & vbcrlf)")
            for Each prop in obj~Properties_
                txtstream~WriteLine("Response.Write(""<td>" || GetValue(prop~Name,
obj) || "</td>""" & vbcrlf)")
            next
            txtstream~WriteLine("Response.Write(""</tr>""" & vbcrlf)")
        Next
        txtstream~WriteLine("%>")
        txtstream~WriteLine(</table>")
        txtstream~WriteLine("</body>")
        txtstream~WriteLine("</html>")
        txtstream~close
```

For Single Line Vertical

```
        txtstream~WriteLine("<html>")
        txtstream~WriteLine("<head>")
        txtstream~WriteLine("<style type='text/css'>")
        txtstream~WriteLine("th")
        txtstream~WriteLine("{")
        txtstream~WriteLine("   COLOR: darkred;")
        txtstream~WriteLine("   BACKGROUND-COLOR: white;")
        txtstream~WriteLine("   FONT-FAMILY: font-family: Cambria, serif;")
        txtstream~WriteLine("   FONT-SIZE: 12px;")
        txtstream~WriteLine("   text-align: left;")
        txtstream~WriteLine("   white-Space: nowrap;")
        txtstream~WriteLine("}")
        txtstream~WriteLine("td")
        txtstream~WriteLine("{")
```

```
txtstream~WriteLine("    COLOR: navy;")
txtstream~WriteLine("    BACKGROUND-COLOR: white;")
txtstream~WriteLine("    FONT-FAMILY: font-family: Cambria, serif;")
txtstream~WriteLine("    FONT-SIZE: 12px;")
txtstream~WriteLine("    text-align: left;")
txtstream~WriteLine("    white-Space: nowrap;")
txtstream~WriteLine("}")
txtstream~WriteLine("</style>")
txtstream~WriteLine("<title>Win32_Process</title>")
txtstream~WriteLine("</head>")
txtstream~WriteLine("<body>")
```

Use this if you want to create a border around your table:
```
txtstream~WriteLine("<table Border='1' cellpadding='1' cellspacing='1'>")
```

Use this if you don't want to create a border around your table:
```
txtstream~WriteLine("<table Border='0' cellpadding='1' cellspacing='1'>")
```

```
txtstream~WriteLine("<%")
obj = objs~ItemIndex(0)
for Each prop in obj~Properties_
    txtstream~WriteLine("Response.Write(""<tr><th>"    ||    prop~Name    ||
"</th>(""""<td>" || GetValue(prop~Name, obj) || "</td></tr>""" & vbcrlf)")
    next
txtstream~WriteLine("%>")
txtstream~WriteLine(</table>")
txtstream~WriteLine("</body>")
txtstream~WriteLine("</html>")
txtstream~close
```

For Multi Line Vertical

```
txtstream~WriteLine("<html>")
```

```
txtstream~WriteLine("<head>")
txtstream~WriteLine("<style type='text/css'>")
txtstream~WriteLine("th")
txtstream~WriteLine("{")
txtstream~WriteLine("    COLOR: darkred;")
txtstream~WriteLine("    BACKGROUND-COLOR: white;")
txtstream~WriteLine("    FONT-FAMILY: font-family: Cambria, serif;")
txtstream~WriteLine("    FONT-SIZE: 12px;")
txtstream~WriteLine("    text-align: left;")
txtstream~WriteLine("    white-Space: nowrap;")
txtstream~WriteLine("}")
txtstream~WriteLine("td")
txtstream~WriteLine("{")
txtstream~WriteLine("    COLOR: navy;")
txtstream~WriteLine("    BACKGROUND-COLOR: white;")
txtstream~WriteLine("    FONT-FAMILY: font-family: Cambria, serif;")
txtstream~WriteLine("    FONT-SIZE: 12px;")
txtstream~WriteLine("    text-align: left;")
txtstream~WriteLine("    white-Space: nowrap;")
txtstream~WriteLine("}")
txtstream~WriteLine("</style>")
txtstream~WriteLine("<title>Win32_Process</title>")
txtstream~WriteLine("</head>")
txtstream~WriteLine("<body>")
```

Use this if you want to create a border around your table:
```
txtstream~WriteLine("<table Border='1' cellpadding='1' cellspacing='1'>")
```

Use this if you don't want to create a border around your table:
```
txtstream~WriteLine("<table Border='0' cellpadding='1' cellspacing='1'>")
txtstream~WriteLine("<%")
obj = objs~ItemIndex(0)
for Each prop in obj~Properties_
```

```
        txtstream~WriteLine("Response.Write("""<tr><th>"    ||    prop~Name    ||
"</th>""" & vbcrlf)")
      For Each obj in objs
        txtstream~WriteLine("Response.Write("""<td>"    ||   GetValue(prop~Name,
obj) || "</td>""" & vbcrlf)")
      next
      txtstream~WriteLine("Response.Write("""</tr>""" & vbcrlf)")
    Next
    txtstream~WriteLine("%>")
    txtstream~WriteLine(</table>")
    txtstream~WriteLine("</body>")
    txtstream~WriteLine("</html>")
    txtstream~close
```

ASPX Code

Below, is the code for ASP.

```
ws = .OLEObject~new("WScript.Shell")
txtstream = fso~OpenTextFile(ws~CurrentDirectory || "\Win32_Process.aspx",
2, true, -2)
```

For Single Line Horizontal

```
txtstream~WriteLine("<!DOCTYPE html PUBLIC ""-//W3C//DTD XHTML 1.0
Transitional//EN"" ""http://www.w3.org/TR/xhtml1/DTD/xhtml1-
transitional.dtd"">")
txtstream~WriteLine("")
txtstream~WriteLine("<html xmlns="http://www.w3.org/1999/xhtml"
>")
txtstream~WriteLine("<head>")
txtstream~WriteLine("<style type='text/css'>")
txtstream~WriteLine("th")
txtstream~WriteLine("{")
txtstream~WriteLine("   COLOR: darkred;")
txtstream~WriteLine("   BACKGROUND-COLOR: white;")
txtstream~WriteLine("   FONT-FAMILY: font-family: Cambria, serif;")
```

```
txtstream~WriteLine("    FONT-SIZE: 12px;")
txtstream~WriteLine("    text-align: left;")
txtstream~WriteLine("    white-Space: nowrap;")
txtstream~WriteLine("}")
txtstream~WriteLine("td")
txtstream~WriteLine("{")
txtstream~WriteLine("    COLOR: navy;")
txtstream~WriteLine("    BACKGROUND-COLOR: white;")
txtstream~WriteLine("    FONT-FAMILY: font-family: Cambria, serif;")
txtstream~WriteLine("    FONT-SIZE: 12px;")
txtstream~WriteLine("    text-align: left;")
txtstream~WriteLine("    white-Space: nowrap;")
txtstream~WriteLine("}")
txtstream~WriteLine("</style>")
txtstream~WriteLine("<title>Win32_Process</title>")
txtstream~WriteLine("</head>")
txtstream~WriteLine("<body>")
```

Use this if you want to create a border around your table:
```
txtstream~WriteLine("<table Border='1' cellpadding='1' cellspacing='1'>")
```

Use this if you don't want to create a border around your table:
```
txtstream~WriteLine("<table Border='0' cellpadding='1' cellspacing='1'>")
txtstream~WriteLine("<%")
obj = objs~ItemIndex(0)
txtstream~WriteLine("Response.Write(""<tr>"" & vbcrlf)")
for Each prop in obj~Properties_
    txtstream~WriteLine("Response.Write(""<th>" || prop~Name || "</th>"" & vbcrlf)")
next
txtstream~WriteLine("Response.Write(""</tr>"" & vbcrlf)")
txtstream~WriteLine("Response.Write(""<tr>"" & vbcrlf)")
for Each prop in obj~Properties_
```

```
txtstream~WriteLine("Response.Write("""<td>" || GetValue(prop~Name, obj)
|| "</td>""" & vbcrlf)")
    next
    txtstream~WriteLine("Response.Write("""</tr>""" & vbcrlf)")
    txtstream~WriteLine("%>")
    txtstream~WriteLine(</table>")
    txtstream~WriteLine("</body>")
    txtstream~WriteLine("</html>")
    txtstream~close
```

For Multi Line Horizontal

```
    txtstream~WriteLine("<!DOCTYPE html PUBLIC """-//W3C//DTD XHTML 1.0
Transitional//EN""" """http://www.w3.org/TR/xhtml1/DTD/xhtml1-
transitional.dtd""">")
    txtstream~WriteLine("")
    txtstream~WriteLine("<html xmlns="http://www.w3.org/1999/xhtml"
>")
    txtstream~WriteLine("<head>")
    txtstream~WriteLine("<style type='text/css'>")
    txtstream~WriteLine("th")
    txtstream~WriteLine("{")
    txtstream~WriteLine("   COLOR: darkred;")
    txtstream~WriteLine("   BACKGROUND-COLOR: white;")
    txtstream~WriteLine("   FONT-FAMILY: font-family: Cambria, serif;")
    txtstream~WriteLine("   FONT-SIZE: 12px;")
    txtstream~WriteLine("   text-align: left;")
    txtstream~WriteLine("   white-Space: nowrap;")
    txtstream~WriteLine("}")
    txtstream~WriteLine("td")
    txtstream~WriteLine("{")
    txtstream~WriteLine("   COLOR: navy;")
    txtstream~WriteLine("   BACKGROUND-COLOR: white;")
    txtstream~WriteLine("   FONT-FAMILY: font-family: Cambria, serif;")
```

```
txtstream~WriteLine("    FONT-SIZE: 12px;")
txtstream~WriteLine("    text-align: left;")
txtstream~WriteLine("    white-Space: nowrap;")
txtstream~WriteLine("}")
txtstream~WriteLine("</style>")
txtstream~WriteLine("<title>Win32_Process</title>")
txtstream~WriteLine("</head>")
txtstream~WriteLine("<body>")
```

Use this if you want to create a border around your table:
```
txtstream~WriteLine("<table Border='1' cellpadding='1' cellspacing='1'>")
```

Use this if you don't want to create a border around your table:
```
txtstream~WriteLine("<table Border='0' cellpadding='1' cellspacing='1'>")
```

```
txtstream~WriteLine("<%")
obj = objs~ItemIndex(0)
txtstream~WriteLine("Response.Write(""<tr>"" & vbcrlf)")
for Each prop in obj~Properties_
    txtstream~WriteLine("Response.Write(""<th>" || prop~Name || "</th>"" & vbcrlf)")
next
txtstream~WriteLine("Response.Write(""</tr>"" & vbcrlf)")
For Each obj in objs
    txtstream~WriteLine("Response.Write(""<tr>"" & vbcrlf)")
    for Each prop in obj~Properties_
        txtstream~WriteLine("Response.Write(""<td>" || GetValue(prop~Name, obj) || "</td>"" & vbcrlf)")
    next
    txtstream~WriteLine("Response.Write(""</tr>"" & vbcrlf)")
Next
txtstream~WriteLine("%>")
txtstream~WriteLine(</table>")
```

```
txtstream~WriteLine("</body>")
txtstream~WriteLine("</html>")
txtstream~close
```

For Single Line Vertical

```
txtstream~WriteLine("<!DOCTYPE html PUBLIC ""-//W3C//DTD XHTML 1.0
Transitional//EN"" ""http://www.w3.org/TR/xhtml1/DTD/xhtml1-
transitional.dtd"">")
txtstream~WriteLine("")
txtstream~WriteLine("<html xmlns="http://www.w3.org/1999/xhtml"
>")
txtstream~WriteLine("<head>")
txtstream~WriteLine("<style type='text/css'>")
txtstream~WriteLine("th")
txtstream~WriteLine("{")
txtstream~WriteLine("    COLOR: darkred;")
txtstream~WriteLine("    BACKGROUND-COLOR: white;")
txtstream~WriteLine("    FONT-FAMILY: font-family: Cambria, serif;")
txtstream~WriteLine("    FONT-SIZE: 12px;")
txtstream~WriteLine("    text-align: left;")
txtstream~WriteLine("    white-Space: nowrap;")
txtstream~WriteLine("}")
txtstream~WriteLine("td")
txtstream~WriteLine("{")
txtstream~WriteLine("    COLOR: navy;")
txtstream~WriteLine("    BACKGROUND-COLOR: white;")
txtstream~WriteLine("    FONT-FAMILY: font-family: Cambria, serif;")
txtstream~WriteLine("    FONT-SIZE: 12px;")
txtstream~WriteLine("    text-align: left;")
txtstream~WriteLine("    white-Space: nowrap;")
txtstream~WriteLine("}")
txtstream~WriteLine("</style>")
txtstream~WriteLine("<title>Win32_Process</title>")
txtstream~WriteLine("</head>")
```

```
txtstream~WriteLine("<body>")
```

Use this if you want to create a border around your table:
```
txtstream~WriteLine("<table Border='1' cellpadding='1' cellspacing='1'>")
```

Use this if you don't want to create a border around your table:
```
txtstream~WriteLine("<table Border='0' cellpadding='1' cellspacing='1'>")
```

```
txtstream~WriteLine("<%")
obj = objs~ItemIndex(0)
for Each prop in obj~Properties_
    txtstream~WriteLine("Response.Write(""<tr><th>"    ||    prop~Name    ||
"</th>(""""<td>" || GetValue(prop~Name, obj) || "</td></tr>"" & vbcrlf)")
    next
txtstream~WriteLine("%>")
txtstream~WriteLine(</table>")
txtstream~WriteLine("</body>")
txtstream~WriteLine("</html>")
txtstream~close
```

For Multi Line Vertical

```
txtstream~WriteLine("<!DOCTYPE html PUBLIC ""-//W3C//DTD XHTML 1.0
Transitional//EN"" ""http://www.w3.org/TR/xhtml1/DTD/xhtml1-
transitional.dtd"">")
txtstream~WriteLine("")
txtstream~WriteLine("<html xmlns="http://www.w3.org/1999/xhtml"
>")
txtstream~WriteLine("<head>")
txtstream~WriteLine("<style type='text/css'>")
txtstream~WriteLine("th")
txtstream~WriteLine("{")
txtstream~WriteLine("   COLOR: darkred;")
txtstream~WriteLine("   BACKGROUND-COLOR: white;")
```

```
txtstream~WriteLine("    FONT-FAMILY: font-family: Cambria, serif;")
txtstream~WriteLine("    FONT-SIZE: 12px;")
txtstream~WriteLine("    text-align: left;")
txtstream~WriteLine("    white-Space: nowrap;")
txtstream~WriteLine("}")
txtstream~WriteLine("td")
txtstream~WriteLine("{")
txtstream~WriteLine("    COLOR: navy;")
txtstream~WriteLine("    BACKGROUND-COLOR: white;")
txtstream~WriteLine("    FONT-FAMILY: font-family: Cambria, serif;")
txtstream~WriteLine("    FONT-SIZE: 12px;")
txtstream~WriteLine("    text-align: left;")
txtstream~WriteLine("    white-Space: nowrap;")
txtstream~WriteLine("}")
txtstream~WriteLine("</style>")
txtstream~WriteLine("<title>Win32_Process</title>")
txtstream~WriteLine("</head>")
txtstream~WriteLine("<body>")
```

Use this if you want to create a border around your table:
```
txtstream~WriteLine("<table Border='1' cellpadding='1' cellspacing='1'>")
```

Use this if you don't want to create a border around your table:
```
txtstream~WriteLine("<table Border='0' cellpadding='1' cellspacing='1'>")
```

```
txtstream~WriteLine("<%")
obj = objs~ItemIndex(0)
for Each prop in obj~Properties_
    txtstream~WriteLine("Response.Write(""<tr><th>"    ||    prop~Name    ||
"</th>""" & vbcrlf)")
        For Each obj in objs
            txtstream~WriteLine("Response.Write(""<td>"   ||  GetValue(prop~Name,
obj) || "</td>""" & vbcrlf)")
```

```
    next
    txtstream~WriteLine("Response.Write(""</tr>"" & vbcrlf)")
Next
txtstream~WriteLine("%>")
txtstream~WriteLine(</table>")
txtstream~WriteLine("</body>")
txtstream~WriteLine("</html>")
txtstream~close
```

HTA Code

B elow, is the code for HTA.

```
ws = .OLEObject~new("WScript.Shell")
txtstream = fso~OpenTextFile(ws~CurrentDirectory || "\Win32_Process.hta",
2, true, -2)
```

For Single Line Horizontal

```
txtstream~WriteLine("<html>")
txtstream~WriteLine("<head>")
txtstream~WriteLine("<HTA:APPLICATION ")
txtstream~WriteLine("ID = ""Process"" ")
txtstream~WriteLine("APPLICATIONNAME = ""Process"" ")
txtstream~WriteLine("SCROLL = ""yes"" ")
txtstream~WriteLine("SINGLEINSTANCE = ""yes"" ")
txtstream~WriteLine("WINDOWSTATE = ""maximize"" >")
txtstream~WriteLine("<style type='text/css'>")
txtstream~WriteLine("th")
txtstream~WriteLine("{")
```

```
txtstream~WriteLine("    COLOR: darkred;")
txtstream~WriteLine("    BACKGROUND-COLOR: white;")
txtstream~WriteLine("    FONT-FAMILY: font-family: Cambria, serif;")
txtstream~WriteLine("    FONT-SIZE: 12px;")
txtstream~WriteLine("    text-align: left;")
txtstream~WriteLine("    white-Space: nowrap;")
txtstream~WriteLine("}")
txtstream~WriteLine("td")
txtstream~WriteLine("{")
txtstream~WriteLine("    COLOR: navy;")
txtstream~WriteLine("    BACKGROUND-COLOR: white;")
txtstream~WriteLine("    FONT-FAMILY: font-family: Cambria, serif;")
txtstream~WriteLine("    FONT-SIZE: 12px;")
txtstream~WriteLine("    text-align: left;")
txtstream~WriteLine("    white-Space: nowrap;")
txtstream~WriteLine("}")
txtstream~WriteLine("</style>")
txtstream~WriteLine("<title>Win32_Process</title>")
txtstream~WriteLine("</head>")
txtstream~WriteLine("<body>")
```

Use this if you want to create a border around your table:

```
txtstream~WriteLine("<table Border='1' cellpadding='1' cellspacing='1'>")
```

Use this if you don't want to create a border around your table:

```
txtstream~WriteLine("<table Border='0' cellpadding='1' cellspacing='1'>")
obj = objs~ItemIndex(0)
txtstream~WriteLine("<tr>)")
for Each prop in obj~Properties_
    txtstream~WriteLine("<th>" || prop~Name || "</th>)")
next
txtstream~WriteLine("</tr>)")
txtstream~WriteLine("<tr>)")
```

```
for Each prop in obj~Properties_
    txtstream~WriteLine("<td>" || GetValue(prop~Name, obj) || "</td>)")
next
txtstream~WriteLine("</tr>)")
txtstream~WriteLine(</table>")
txtstream~WriteLine("</body>")
txtstream~WriteLine("</html>")
txtstream~close
```

For Multi Line Horizontal

```
txtstream~WriteLine(html>")
txtstream~WriteLine("<head>")
txtstream~WriteLine("<HTA:APPLICATION ")
txtstream~WriteLine("ID = ""Process"" ")
txtstream~WriteLine("APPLICATIONNAME = ""Process"" ")
txtstream~WriteLine("SCROLL = ""yes"" ")
txtstream~WriteLine("SINGLEINSTANCE = ""yes"" ")
txtstream~WriteLine("WINDOWSTATE = ""maximize"" >")
txtstream~WriteLine("<style type='text/css'>")
txtstream~WriteLine("th")
txtstream~WriteLine("{")
txtstream~WriteLine("    COLOR: darkred;")
txtstream~WriteLine("    BACKGROUND-COLOR: white;")
txtstream~WriteLine("    FONT-FAMILY: font-family: Cambria, serif;")
txtstream~WriteLine("    FONT-SIZE: 12px;")
txtstream~WriteLine("    text-align: left;")
txtstream~WriteLine("    white-Space: nowrap;")
txtstream~WriteLine("}")
txtstream~WriteLine("td")
txtstream~WriteLine("{")
txtstream~WriteLine("    COLOR: navy;")
txtstream~WriteLine("    BACKGROUND-COLOR: white;")
```

```
txtstream~WriteLine("    FONT-FAMILY: font-family: Cambria, serif;")
txtstream~WriteLine("    FONT-SIZE: 12px;")
txtstream~WriteLine("    text-align: left;")
txtstream~WriteLine("    white-Space: nowrap;")
txtstream~WriteLine("}")
txtstream~WriteLine("</style>")
txtstream~WriteLine("<title>Win32_Process</title>")
txtstream~WriteLine("</head>")
txtstream~WriteLine("<body>")
```

Use this if you want to create a border around your table:
```
txtstream~WriteLine("<table Border='1' cellpadding='1' cellspacing='1'>")
```

Use this if you don't want to create a border around your table:
```
txtstream~WriteLine("<table Border='0' cellpadding='1' cellspacing='1'>")
```

```
obj = objs~ItemIndex(0)
txtstream~WriteLine("<tr>)")
for Each prop in obj~Properties_
   txtstream~WriteLine("<th>" || prop~Name || "</th>)")
next
txtstream~WriteLine("</tr>)")
For Each obj in objs
   txtstream~WriteLine("<tr>)")
   for Each prop in obj~Properties_
      txtstream~WriteLine("<td>" || GetValue(prop~Name, obj) || "</td>)")
   next
   txtstream~WriteLine("</tr>)")
Next
txtstream~WriteLine(</table>")
txtstream~WriteLine("</body>")
txtstream~WriteLine("</html>")
txtstream~close
```

For Single Line Vertical

```
txtstream~WriteLine("<html>")
txtstream~WriteLine("<head>")
txtstream~WriteLine("<HTA:APPLICATION ")
txtstream~WriteLine("ID = ""Process"" ")
txtstream~WriteLine("APPLICATIONNAME = ""Process"" ")
txtstream~WriteLine("SCROLL = ""yes"" ")
txtstream~WriteLine("SINGLEINSTANCE = ""yes"" ")
txtstream~WriteLine("WINDOWSTATE = ""maximize"" >")
txtstream~WriteLine("<style type='text/css'>")
txtstream~WriteLine("th")
txtstream~WriteLine("{")
txtstream~WriteLine("    COLOR: darkred;")
txtstream~WriteLine("    BACKGROUND-COLOR: white;")
txtstream~WriteLine("    FONT-FAMILY: font-family: Cambria, serif;")
txtstream~WriteLine("    FONT-SIZE: 12px;")
txtstream~WriteLine("    text-align: left;")
txtstream~WriteLine("    white-Space: nowrap;")
txtstream~WriteLine("}")
txtstream~WriteLine("td")
txtstream~WriteLine("{")
txtstream~WriteLine("    COLOR: navy;")
txtstream~WriteLine("    BACKGROUND-COLOR: white;")
txtstream~WriteLine("    FONT-FAMILY: font-family: Cambria, serif;")
txtstream~WriteLine("    FONT-SIZE: 12px;")
txtstream~WriteLine("    text-align: left;")
txtstream~WriteLine("    white-Space: nowrap;")
txtstream~WriteLine("}")
txtstream~WriteLine("</style>")
txtstream~WriteLine("<title>Win32_Process</title>")
```

```
txtstream~WriteLine("</head>")
txtstream~WriteLine("<body>")
```

Use this if you want to create a border around your table:
```
txtstream~WriteLine("<table Border='1' cellpadding='1' cellspacing='1'>")
```

Use this if you don't want to create a border around your table:
```
txtstream~WriteLine("<table Border='0' cellpadding='1' cellspacing='1'>")
```

```
obj = objs~ItemIndex(0)
for Each prop in obj~Properties_
    txtstream~WriteLine("<tr><th>" || prop~Name || "</th>(""<td>" || GetValue(prop~Name, obj) || "</td></tr>)")
next
txtstream~WriteLine(</table>")
txtstream~WriteLine("</body>")
txtstream~WriteLine("</html>")
txtstream~close
```

For Multi Line Vertical

```
txtstream~WriteLine("<html>")
txtstream~WriteLine("<head>")
txtstream~WriteLine("<HTA:APPLICATION ")
txtstream~WriteLine("ID = ""Process"" ")
txtstream~WriteLine("APPLICATIONNAME = ""Process"" ")
txtstream~WriteLine("SCROLL = ""yes"" ")
txtstream~WriteLine("SINGLEINSTANCE = ""yes"" ")
txtstream~WriteLine("WINDOWSTATE = ""maximize"" >")

txtstream~WriteLine("<style type='text/css'>")
txtstream~WriteLine("th")
txtstream~WriteLine("{")
txtstream~WriteLine("    COLOR: darkred;")
```

```
txtstream~WriteLine("    BACKGROUND-COLOR: white;")
txtstream~WriteLine("    FONT-FAMILY: font-family: Cambria, serif;")
txtstream~WriteLine("    FONT-SIZE: 12px;")
txtstream~WriteLine("    text-align: left;")
txtstream~WriteLine("    white-Space: nowrap;")
txtstream~WriteLine("}")
txtstream~WriteLine("td")
txtstream~WriteLine("{")
txtstream~WriteLine("    COLOR: navy;")
txtstream~WriteLine("    BACKGROUND-COLOR: white;")
txtstream~WriteLine("    FONT-FAMILY: font-family: Cambria, serif;")
txtstream~WriteLine("    FONT-SIZE: 12px;")
txtstream~WriteLine("    text-align: left;")
txtstream~WriteLine("    white-Space: nowrap;")
txtstream~WriteLine("}")
txtstream~WriteLine("</style>")
txtstream~WriteLine("<title>Win32_Process</title>")
txtstream~WriteLine("</head>")
txtstream~WriteLine("<body>")
```

Use this if you want to create a border around your table:
```
txtstream~WriteLine("<table Border='1' cellpadding='1' cellspacing='1'>")
```

Use this if you don't want to create a border around your table:
```
txtstream~WriteLine("<table Border='0' cellpadding='1' cellspacing='1'>")
obj = objs~ItemIndex(0)
for Each prop in obj~Properties_
    txtstream~WriteLine("<tr><th>" || prop~Name || "</th>)")
    For Each obj in objs
        txtstream~WriteLine("<td>" || GetValue(prop~Name, obj) || "</td>)")
    next
    txtstream~WriteLine("</tr>)")
Next
```

```
txtstream~WriteLine("</table>")
txtstream~WriteLine("</body>")
txtstream~WriteLine("</html>")
txtstream~close
```

HTML Code

B elow, is the code for HTML.

```
ws = .OLEObject~new("WScript.Shell")
txtstream = fso~OpenTextFile(ws~CurrentDirectory || "\Win32_Process.html",
2, true, -2)
```

For Single Line Horizontal

```
txtstream~WriteLine("<html>")
txtstream~WriteLine("<head>")
txtstream~WriteLine("<style type='text/css'>")
txtstream~WriteLine("th")
txtstream~WriteLine("{")
txtstream~WriteLine("    COLOR: darkred;")
txtstream~WriteLine("    BACKGROUND-COLOR: white;")
txtstream~WriteLine("    FONT-FAMILY: font-family: Cambria, serif;")
txtstream~WriteLine("    FONT-SIZE: 12px;")
txtstream~WriteLine("    text-align: left;")
txtstream~WriteLine("    white-Space: nowrap;")
```

```
txtstream~WriteLine("}")
txtstream~WriteLine("td")
txtstream~WriteLine("{")
txtstream~WriteLine("   COLOR: navy;")
txtstream~WriteLine("   BACKGROUND-COLOR: white;")
txtstream~WriteLine("   FONT-FAMILY: font-family: Cambria, serif;")
txtstream~WriteLine("   FONT-SIZE: 12px;")
txtstream~WriteLine("   text-align: left;")
txtstream~WriteLine("   white-Space: nowrap;")
txtstream~WriteLine("}")
txtstream~WriteLine("</style>")
txtstream~WriteLine("<title>Win32_Process</title>")
txtstream~WriteLine("</head>")
txtstream~WriteLine("<body>")
```

Use this if you want to create a border around your table:
```
txtstream~WriteLine("<table Border='1' cellpadding='1' cellspacing='1'>")
```

Use this if you don't want to create a border around your table:
```
txtstream~WriteLine("<table Border='0' cellpadding='1' cellspacing='1'>")
obj = objs~ItemIndex(0)
txtstream~WriteLine("<tr>)")
for Each prop in obj~Properties_
   txtstream~WriteLine("<th>" || prop~Name || "</th>)")
next
txtstream~WriteLine("</tr>)")
txtstream~WriteLine("<tr>)")
for Each prop in obj~Properties_
   txtstream~WriteLine("<td>" || GetValue(prop~Name, obj) || "</td>)")
next
txtstream~WriteLine("</tr>)")
txtstream~WriteLine(</table>")
txtstream~WriteLine("</body>")
```

txtstream~WriteLine("</html>")

txtstream~close

For Multi Line Horizontal

txtstream~WriteLine(html>")

txtstream~WriteLine("<head>")

txtstream~WriteLine("<style type='text/css'>")

txtstream~WriteLine("th")

txtstream~WriteLine("{")

txtstream~WriteLine("   COLOR: darkred;")

txtstream~WriteLine("   BACKGROUND-COLOR: white;")

txtstream~WriteLine("   FONT-FAMILY: font-family: Cambria, serif;")

txtstream~WriteLine("   FONT-SIZE: 12px;")

txtstream~WriteLine("   text-align: left;")

txtstream~WriteLine("   white-Space: nowrap;")

txtstream~WriteLine("}")

txtstream~WriteLine("td")

txtstream~WriteLine("{")

txtstream~WriteLine("   COLOR: navy;")

txtstream~WriteLine("   BACKGROUND-COLOR: white;")

txtstream~WriteLine("   FONT-FAMILY: font-family: Cambria, serif;")

txtstream~WriteLine("   FONT-SIZE: 12px;")

txtstream~WriteLine("   text-align: left;")

txtstream~WriteLine("   white-Space: nowrap;")

txtstream~WriteLine("}")

txtstream~WriteLine("</style>")

txtstream~WriteLine("<title>Win32_Process</title>")

txtstream~WriteLine("</head>")

txtstream~WriteLine("<body>")

Use this if you want to create a border around your table:

txtstream~WriteLine("<table Border='1' cellpadding='1' cellspacing='1'>")

Use this if you don't want to create a border around your table:

```
txtstream~WriteLine("<table Border='0' cellpadding='1' cellspacing='1'>")

obj = objs~ItemIndex(0)
txtstream~WriteLine("<tr>)")
for Each prop in obj~Properties_
    txtstream~WriteLine("<th>" || prop~Name || "</th>)")
next
txtstream~WriteLine("</tr>)")
For Each obj in objs
    txtstream~WriteLine("<tr>)")
    for Each prop in obj~Properties_
        txtstream~WriteLine("<td>" || GetValue(prop~Name, obj) || "</td>)")
    next
    txtstream~WriteLine("</tr>)")
Next
txtstream~WriteLine(</table>")
txtstream~WriteLine("</body>")
txtstream~WriteLine("</html>")
txtstream~close
```

For Single Line Vertical

```
txtstream~WriteLine("<html>")
txtstream~WriteLine("<style type='text/css'>")
txtstream~WriteLine("th")
txtstream~WriteLine("{")
txtstream~WriteLine("   COLOR: darkred;")
txtstream~WriteLine("   BACKGROUND-COLOR: white;")
txtstream~WriteLine("   FONT-FAMILY: font-family: Cambria, serif;")
txtstream~WriteLine("   FONT-SIZE: 12px;")
```

```
txtstream~WriteLine("    text-align: left;")
txtstream~WriteLine("    white-Space: nowrap;")
txtstream~WriteLine("}")
txtstream~WriteLine("td")
txtstream~WriteLine("{")
txtstream~WriteLine("    COLOR: navy;")
txtstream~WriteLine("    BACKGROUND-COLOR: white;")
txtstream~WriteLine("    FONT-FAMILY: font-family: Cambria, serif;")
txtstream~WriteLine("    FONT-SIZE: 12px;")
txtstream~WriteLine("    text-align: left;")
txtstream~WriteLine("    white-Space: nowrap;")
txtstream~WriteLine("}")
txtstream~WriteLine("</style>")
txtstream~WriteLine("<title>Win32_Process</title>")
txtstream~WriteLine("</head>")
txtstream~WriteLine("<body>")
```

Use this if you want to create a border around your table:
```
txtstream~WriteLine("<table Border='1' cellpadding='1' cellspacing='1'>")
```

Use this if you don't want to create a border around your table:
```
txtstream~WriteLine("<table Border='0' cellpadding='1' cellspacing='1'>")
```

```
obj = objs~ItemIndex(0)
for Each prop in obj~Properties_
    txtstream~WriteLine("<tr><th>" || prop~Name || "</th>(""<td>" || GetValue(prop~Name, obj) || "</td></tr>)")
next
txtstream~WriteLine(</table>")
txtstream~WriteLine("</body>")
txtstream~WriteLine("</html>")
txtstream~close
```

For Multi Line Vertical

```
txtstream~WriteLine("<html>")
txtstream~WriteLine("<head>")
txtstream~WriteLine("<style type='text/css'>")
txtstream~WriteLine("th")
txtstream~WriteLine("{")
txtstream~WriteLine("   COLOR: darkred;")
txtstream~WriteLine("   BACKGROUND-COLOR: white;")
txtstream~WriteLine("   FONT-FAMILY: font-family: Cambria, serif;")
txtstream~WriteLine("   FONT-SIZE: 12px;")
txtstream~WriteLine("   text-align: left;")
txtstream~WriteLine("   white-Space: nowrap;")
txtstream~WriteLine("}")
txtstream~WriteLine("td")
txtstream~WriteLine("{")
txtstream~WriteLine("   COLOR: navy;")
txtstream~WriteLine("   BACKGROUND-COLOR: white;")
txtstream~WriteLine("   FONT-FAMILY: font-family: Cambria, serif;")
txtstream~WriteLine("   FONT-SIZE: 12px;")
txtstream~WriteLine("   text-align: left;")
txtstream~WriteLine("   white-Space: nowrap;")
txtstream~WriteLine("}")
txtstream~WriteLine("</style>")
txtstream~WriteLine("<title>Win32_Process</title>")
txtstream~WriteLine("</head>")
txtstream~WriteLine("<body>")
```

Use this if you want to create a border around your table:
```
txtstream~WriteLine("<table Border='1' cellpadding='1' cellspacing='1'>")
```

Use this if you don't want to create a border around your table:
```
txtstream~WriteLine("<table Border='0' cellpadding='1' cellspacing='1'>")
obj = objs~ItemIndex(0)
```

```
for Each prop in obj~Properties_
    txtstream~WriteLine("<tr><th>" || prop~Name || "</th>)")
    For Each obj in objs
        txtstream~WriteLine("<td>" || GetValue(prop~Name, obj) || "</td>)")
    next
    txtstream~WriteLine("</tr>)")
Next
txtstream~WriteLine(</table>")
txtstream~WriteLine("</body>")
txtstream~WriteLine("</html>")
txtstream~close
```

Text Delimited File Examples

Text files can be databases, too

B elow, are code samples for creating various types of delimited files.

```
quote = '22'x
```

Colon Delimited

```
tempstr = ""
ws = .OLEObject~new("WScript.Shell")
fso = .OLEObject~new("Scripting.FileSystemObject")
txtstream = fso~OpenTextFile(ws~CurrentDirectory || "\Win32_Process.txt" ,
2, true, -2)
```

HORIZONTAL

```
obj = objs~ItemIndex(0)
For Each prop in obj~Properties_
```

```
    if(tempstr <> "")
      tempstr = tempstr || ":"
    Endif
    tempstr = tempstr || prop~Name
  Next
  txtstream~WriteLine(tempstr)
  For Each obj in objs
    For Each prop in obj~Properties_
      if(tempstr <> "")
        tempstr = tempstr  || ":"
      Endif
      tempstr = tempstr || quote || GetValue(prop~Name, obj) || quote
    Next
    txtstream~WriteLine(tempstr)
    tempstr = ""
  Next
  txtstream~close
```

VERTICAL

```
obj = objs~ItemIndex(0)
For Each prop in obj~Properties_
  tempstr = prop~Name
  For Each obj in objs
    if(tempstr <> "")
      tempstr = tempstr  || ":"
    Endif
    tempstr = tempstr || quote || GetValue(prop~Name, obj) || quote
  Next
  txtstream~WriteLine(tempstr)
  tempstr = ""
```

```
Next
txtstream~close
```

Comma Delimited

```
tempstr = ""
ws = .OLEObject~new("WScript.Shell")
fso = .OLEObject~new("Scripting.FileSystemObject")
txtstream = fso~OpenTextFile(ws~CurrentDirectory || "\Win32_Process.csv" ,
2, true, -2)
```

HORIZONTAL

```
obj = objs~ItemIndex(0)
For Each prop in obj~Properties_
    if(tempstr <> "")
        tempstr = tempstr || ","
    Endif
    tempstr = tempstr || prop~Name
Next
txtstream~WriteLine(tempstr)
For Each obj in objs
    For Each prop in obj~Properties_
        if(tempstr <> "")
            tempstr = tempstr || ","
        Endif
        tempstr = tempstr || quote || GetValue(prop~Name, obj) || quote
    Next
    txtstream~WriteLine(tempstr)
    tempstr = ""
Next
```

```
    txtstream~close
```

VERTICAL

```
obj = objs~ItemIndex(0)
For Each prop in obj~Properties_
    tempstr = prop~Name
    For Each obj in objs
        if(tempstr <> "")
            tempstr = tempstr || ","
        Endif
        tempstr = tempstr || quote || GetValue(prop~Name, obj) || quote
    Next
    txtstream~WriteLine(tempstr)
    tempstr = ""
Next
txtstream~close
```

Exclamation Delimited

```
    tempstr = ""
    ws = .OLEObject~new("WScript.Shell")
    fso = .OLEObject~new("Scripting.FileSystemObject")
    txtstream = fso~OpenTextFile(ws~CurrentDirectory || "\Win32_Process.txt",
2, true, -2)
```

HORIZONTAL

```
obj = objs~ItemIndex(0)
For Each prop in obj~Properties_
   if(tempstr <> "")
      tempstr = tempstr || "!"
   Endif
   tempstr = tempstr || prop~Name
Next
txtstream~WriteLine(tempstr)
For Each obj in objs
   For Each prop in obj~Properties_
      if(tempstr <> "")
         tempstr = tempstr  || "!"
      Endif
      tempstr = tempstr || quote ||  GetValue(prop~Name, obj) || quote
   Next
   txtstream~WriteLine(tempstr)
   tempstr = ""
Next
txtstream~close
```

VERTICAL

```
obj = objs~ItemIndex(0)
For Each prop in obj~Properties_
   tempstr = prop~Name
   For Each obj in objs
      if(tempstr <> "")
         tempstr = tempstr  || "!"
      Endif
      tempstr = tempstr || quote ||  GetValue(prop~Name, obj) || quote
```

```
      Next
      txtstream~WriteLine(tempstr)
      tempstr = ""
    Next
    txtstream~close
```

SEMI COLON

```
    tempstr = ""
    ws = .OLEObject~new("WScript.Shell")
    fso = .OLEObject~new("Scripting.FileSystemObject")
    txtstream = fso~OpenTextFile(ws~CurrentDirectory || "\Win32_Process.txt",
2, true, -2)
```

HORIZONTAL

```
    obj = objs~ItemIndex(0)
    For Each prop in obj~Properties_
       if(tempstr <> "")
          tempstr = tempstr || ";"
       Endif
       tempstr = tempstr || prop~Name
    Next
    txtstream~WriteLine(tempstr)
    For Each obj in objs
       For Each prop in obj~Properties_
          if(tempstr <> "")
             tempstr = tempstr || ";"
          Endif
          tempstr = tempstr  chr(34) || GetValue(prop~Name, obj) || chr(34)
```

```
        Next
        txtstream~WriteLine(tempstr)
        tempstr = ""
    Next
    txtstream~close
```

VERTICAL

```
    obj = objs~ItemIndex(0)
    For Each prop in obj~Properties_
        tempstr = prop~Name
        For Each obj in objs
            if(tempstr <> "")
                tempstr = tempstr || ";"
            Endif
            tempstr = tempstr || quote || GetValue(prop~Name, obj) || quote
        Next
        txtstream~WriteLine(tempstr)
        tempstr = ""
    Next
    txtstream~close
```

Tab Delimited

```
    tempstr = ""
    ws = .OLEObject~new("WScript.Shell")
    fso = .OLEObject~new("Scripting.FileSystemObject")
    txtstream = fso~OpenTextFile(ws~CurrentDirectory || "\Win32_Process.txt",
2, true, -2)
```

HORIZONTAL

```
obj = objs~ItemIndex(0)
For Each prop in obj~Properties_
   if(tempstr <> "")
      tempstr = tempstr || vbtab
   Endif
   tempstr = tempstr || prop~Name
Next
txtstream~WriteLine(tempstr)
For Each obj in objs
   For Each prop in obj~Properties_
      if(tempstr <> "")
         tempstr = tempstr || vbtab
      Endif
      tempstr = tempstr || quote || GetValue(prop~Name, obj) || quote
   Next
   txtstream~WriteLine(tempstr)
   tempstr = ""
Next
txtstream~close
```

VERTICAL

```
obj = objs~ItemIndex(0)
For Each prop in obj~Properties_
   tempstr = prop~Name
   For Each obj in objs
      if(tempstr <> "")
```

```
        tempstr = tempstr || vbtab
      Endif
      tempstr = tempstr || quote || GetValue(prop~Name, obj) || quote
    Next
    txtstream~WriteLine(tempstr)
    tempstr = ""
  Next
  txtstream~close
```

Tilde Delimited

```
  tempstr = ""
  ws = .OLEObject~new("WScript.Shell")
  fso = .OLEObject~new("Scripting.FileSystemObject")
  txtstream = fso~OpenTextFile(ws~CurrentDirectory || "\Win32_Process.txt",
2, true, -2)
```

```
  obj = objs~ItemIndex(0)
  For Each prop in obj~Properties_
    if(tempstr <> "")
      tempstr = tempstr || "~"
    Endif
    tempstr = tempstr || prop~Name
  Next
  txtstream~WriteLine(tempstr)
  For Each obj in objs
    For Each prop in obj~Properties_
      if(tempstr <> "")
        tempstr = tempstr || "~"
```

```
      Endif
      tempstr = tempstr || quote || GetValue(prop~Name, obj) || quote
   Next
   txtstream~WriteLine(tempstr)
   tempstr = ""
Next
txtstream~close
```

VERTICAL

```
obj = objs~ItemIndex(0)
For Each prop in obj~Properties_
   tempstr = prop~Name
   For Each obj in objs
      if(tempstr <> "~")
         tempstr = tempstr || vbtab
      Endif
      tempstr = tempstr || quote || GetValue(prop~Name, obj) || quote
   Next
   txtstream~WriteLine(tempstr)
   tempstr = ""
Next

txtstream~close
```

THE XML FILES

Because they are out there

ELL, I THOUGHT IT WAS CATCHY. Below, are examples of different types of XML that can be used with the MSDAOSP and MSPERSIST Providers. Element XML as a standalone -no XSL referenced – can be used with the MSDAOSP Provider and Schema XML can be used with MSPersist.

Element XML

```
ws = .OLEObject~new("WScript.Shell")
txtstream = fso~OpenTextFile(ws~CurrentDirectory || "\Win32_Process.xml",
2, true, -2)
txtstream~WriteLine("<?xml version='1.0' encoding='iso-8859-1'?>")
txtstream~WriteLine("<data>")
For Each obj in objs
   txtstream~WriteLine("<" || Tablename || ">")
   for Each prop in obj~Properties_
      txtstream~WriteLine("<" || prop~Name || ">" || GetValue(prop~Name,
obj) || "</" || prop~Name || ">")
      next
```

```
        txtstream~WriteLine("</" || Tablename || ">")
    next
    txtstream~WriteLine("</data>")
    txtstream~close
```

WMI to Element XML For XSL

```
    ws = .OLEObject~new("WScript.Shell")
    txtstream = fso~OpenTextFile(ws~CurrentDirectory || "\Win32_Process.xml",
2, true, -2)
    txtstream~WriteLine("<?xml version='1.0' encoding='iso-8859-1'?>")
    txtstream~WriteLine("<?xml-stylesheet    type='Text/xsl'    href="""    ||
ws~CurrentDirectory || "\Win32_Process.xsl"""?>")
    txtstream~WriteLine("<data>")
    For Each obj in objs
        txtstream~WriteLine("<" || Tablename || ">")
        for Each prop in obj~Properties_
            txtstream~WriteLine("<" || prop~Name || ">" || GetValue(prop~Name,
obj)|| "</" || prop~Name || ">")
            next
        txtstream~WriteLine("</" || Tablename || ">")
    next
    txtstream~WriteLine("</data>")
    txtstream~close
```

SCHEMA XML

```
    ws = .OLEObject~new("WScript.Shell")
    txtstream = fso~OpenTextFile(ws~CurrentDirectory || "\Win32_Process.xml",
2, true, -2)
    txtstream~WriteLine("<?xml version='1.0' encoding='iso-8859-1'?>")
```

```
txtstream~WriteLine("<data>")
For Each obj in objs
   txtstream~WriteLine("<" || Tablename || ">")
   for Each prop in obj~Properties_
      txtstream~WriteLine("<" || prop~Name || ">" || GetValue(prop~Name,
obj)|| "</" || prop~Name || ">")
      next
   txtstream~WriteLine("</" || Tablename || ">")
next
txtstream~WriteLine("</data>")
txtstream~close


rs1 = .OLEObject~new("ADODB.Recordvar")
rs1.ActiveConnection          =          "Provider=MSDAOSP;          Data
Source=msxml2.DSOControl"
rs1.Open(ws~CurrentDirectory || "\Win32_Process.xml")


if(fso~FileExists(ws~CurrentDirectory || "\Win32_Process_Schema.xml") =
true)
   fso~DeleteFile(ws~CurrentDirectory || "\Win32_Process_Schema.xml")
Endif
rs1.Save(ws~CurrentDirectory || "\Win32_Process_Schema.xml, 1)
```

EXCEL
Three ways to get the job done

THERE ARE THREE WAYS TO PUT DATA INTO EXCEL. CREATE A COMA DELIMITED FILE AND THEN USE WS~RUN, THROUGH AUTOMATION AND BY CREATING A PHYSICAL SPREADSHEET. Below are examples of doing exactly that.

Using the comma delimited file

```
tempstr = ""
ws = .OLEObject~new("WScript.Shell")
fso = .OLEObject~new("Scripting.FileSystemObject")
txtstream = fso~OpenTextFile(ws~CurrentDirectory || "\Win32_Process.csv" ,
2, true, -2)
```

HORIZONTAL

```
obj = objs~ItemIndex(0)
For Each prop in obj~Properties_
    if(tempstr <> "")
```

```
        tempstr = tempstr || ","
    Endif
    tempstr = tempstr || prop~Name
Next
txtstream~WriteLine(tempstr)
For Each obj in objs
    For Each prop in obj~Properties_
        if(tempstr <> "")
            tempstr = tempstr || ","
        Endif
        tempstr = tempstr || quote || GetValue(prop~Name, obj) || quote
    Next
    txtstream~WriteLine(tempstr)
    tempstr = ""
Next
txtstream~close
ws~Run(ws~CurrentDirectory || "\Win32_Process.csv")
```

VERTICAL

```
obj = objs~ItemIndex(0)
For Each prop in obj~Properties_
    tempstr = prop~Name
    For Each obj in objs
        if(tempstr <> "")
            tempstr = tempstr || ","
        Endif
        tempstr = tempstr || quote || GetValue(prop~Name, obj) || quote
    Next
    txtstream~WriteLine(tempstr)
    tempstr = ""
```

Next

txtstream~close

ws~Run(ws~CurrentDirectory || "\Win32_Process.csv")

Excel Automation

HORIZONTAL VIEW

```
oExcel = .OLEObject~new("Excel.Application")
oExcel.Visible = True
wb = oExcel~Workbooks~Add()
ws = wb~Worksheets(0)
ws~Name = Tablename
y=2
x=1
obj = objs~ItemIndex(0)
for each prop in obj~Properties_
   ws~Cells~Item(1, x) = prop~Name
   x=x+1
next
x=1
For Each obj in objs
   for Each prop in obj~Properties_)
      ws~Cells~Item(y, x) = GetValue(prop~Name, obj)
      x=x+1
   next
   x= 1
```

```
    y= y+1
next
ws~Columns~HorizontalAlignment = -4131
ws~Columns~AutoFit()
```

FOR A VERTICAL VIEW

```
oExcel = .OLEObject~new("Excel.Application")
oExcel.Visible = True
wb = oExcel~Workbooks~Add()
ws = wb.Worksheets(1)
ws~Name = Tablename
y=2
x=1
obj = objs~ItemIndex(0)
for Each prop in obj~Properties_
   ws~Cells~Item(x, 1) = prop~Name
   x=x+1
next
x=1
For Each obj in objs
   for Each prop in obj~Properties_)
     ws~Cells~Item(x, y) = GetValue(prop~Name, obj)
     x=x+1
   next
   x= 1
   y= y+1
next
ws~Columns~HorizontalAlignment = -4131
ws~Columns~AutoFit()
```

Using A Spreadsheet

```
ws = .OLEObject~new("WScript.Shell")
fso = .OLEObject~new("Scripting.FileSystemObject")
txtstream = fso~OpenTextFile(ws~CurrentDirectory || "\\ProcessExcel.xml", 2,
True, -2)
    txtstream~WriteLine("<?xml version='1.0'?>")
    txtstream~WriteLine("<?mso-application progid='Excel.Sheet'?>")
    txtstream~WriteLine("<Workbook          xmlns='urn:schemas-microsoft-
com:office:spreadsheet'        xmlns:o='urn:schemas-microsoft-com:office:office'
xmlns:x='urn:schemas-microsoft-com:office:excel'          xmlns:ss='urn:schemas-
microsoft-com:office:spreadsheet'        xmlns:html='http://www.w3.org/TR/REC-
html40'>")
    txtstream~WriteLine("       <DocumentProperties     xmlns='urn:schemas-
microsoft-com:office:office'>")
    txtstream~WriteLine("              <Author>Windows User</Author>")
    txtstream~WriteLine("              <LastAuthor>Windows
User</LastAuthor>")
    txtstream~WriteLine("              <Created>2007-11-
27T19:36:16Z</Created>")
    txtstream~WriteLine("              <Version>12.00</Version>")
    txtstream~WriteLine("       </DocumentProperties>")
    txtstream~WriteLine("       <ExcelWorkbook          xmlns='urn:schemas-
microsoft-com:office:excel'>")
    txtstream~WriteLine("
    <WindowHeight>11835</WindowHeight>")
    txtstream~WriteLine("
    <WindowWidth>18960</WindowWidth>")
    txtstream~WriteLine("              <WindowTopX>120</WindowTopX>")
    txtstream~WriteLine("              <WindowTopY>135</WindowTopY>")
```

```
txtstream~WriteLine("
    <ProtectStructure>False</ProtectStructure>")
txtstream~WriteLine("
    <ProtectWindows>False</ProtectWindows>")
txtstream~WriteLine("        </ExcelWorkbook>")
txtstream~WriteLine("        <Styles>")
txtstream~WriteLine("            <Style                ss:ID='Default'
ss:Name='Normal'>")
txtstream~WriteLine("                <Alignment
ss:Vertical='Bottom'/>")
txtstream~WriteLine("                <Borders/>")
txtstream~WriteLine("                <Font    ss:FontName='Calibri'
x:Family='Swiss' ss:Size='11' ss:Color='#000000'/>")
txtstream~WriteLine("                <Interior/>")
txtstream~WriteLine("                <NumberFormat/>")
txtstream~WriteLine("                <Protection/>")
txtstream~WriteLine("            </Style>")
txtstream~WriteLine("            <Style ss:ID='s62'>")
txtstream~WriteLine("                <Borders/>")
txtstream~WriteLine("                <Font    ss:FontName='Calibri'
x:Family='Swiss' ss:Size='11' ss:Color='#000000' ss:Bold='1'/>")
txtstream~WriteLine("            </Style>")
txtstream~WriteLine("            <Style ss:ID='s63'>")
txtstream~WriteLine("                <Alignment
ss:Horizontal='Left' ss:Vertical='Bottom' ss:Indent='2'/>")
txtstream~WriteLine("                <Font    ss:FontName='Verdana'
x:Family='Swiss' ss:Size='7.7' ss:Color='#000000'/>")
txtstream~WriteLine("            </Style>")
txtstream~WriteLine("    </Styles>")
txtstream~WriteLine("<Worksheet ss:Name='Process'>")
txtstream~WriteLine("        <Table    x:FullColumns='1'    x:FullRows='1'
ss:DefaultRowHeight='24.9375'>")
```

```
    txtstream~WriteLine("              <Column ss:AutoFitWidth='1' ss:Width='82.5'
ss:Span='5'/>")
    For Each obj in objs
        txtstream~WriteLine("      <Row ss:AutoFitHeight='0'>")
        For Each prop in obj~Properties_
            txtstream~WriteLine("                       <Cell  ss:StyleID='s62'><Data
ss:Type='String'>" || prop~Name || "</Data></Cell>")
        Next
        txtstream~WriteLine("      </Row>")
        Exit for
    Next


    For Each obj in objs
        txtstream~WriteLine("      <Row ss:AutoFitHeight='0' ss:Height='13.5'>")
        for Each prop in obj~Properties_
            txtstream~WriteLine("        <Cell><Data ss:Type='String'><![CDATA[" ||
GetValue(prop~Name, obj) || "]]></Data></Cell>")
        Next
        txtstream~WriteLine("      </Row>")
    Next
    txtstream~WriteLine("  </Table>")
    txtstream~WriteLine("        <WorksheetOptions          xmlns='urn:schemas-
microsoft-com:office:excel'>")
    txtstream~WriteLine("              <PageSetup>")
    txtstream~WriteLine("                  <Header x:Margin='0.3'/>")
    txtstream~WriteLine("                  <Footer x:Margin='0.3'/>")
    txtstream~WriteLine("                  <PageMargins x:Bottom='0.75'
x:Left='0.7' x:Right='0.7' x:Top='0.75'/>")
    txtstream~WriteLine("              </PageSetup>")
    txtstream~WriteLine("          <Unsynced/>")
    txtstream~WriteLine("          <Print>")
    txtstream~WriteLine("                  <FitHeight>0</FitHeight>")
```

```
txtstream~WriteLine("                              <ValidPrinterInfo/>")
txtstream~WriteLine("
   <HorizontalResolution>600</HorizontalResolution>")
txtstream~WriteLine("
   <VerticalResolution>600</VerticalResolution>")
txtstream~WriteLine("                    </Print>")
txtstream~WriteLine("                    <Selected/>")
txtstream~WriteLine("                    <Panes>")
txtstream~WriteLine("                              <Pane>")
txtstream~WriteLine("
   <Number>3</Number>")
txtstream~WriteLine("
   <ActiveRow>9</ActiveRow>")
txtstream~WriteLine("
   <ActiveCol>7</ActiveCol>")
txtstream~WriteLine("                              </Pane>")
txtstream~WriteLine("                    </Panes>")
txtstream~WriteLine("
   <ProtectObjects>False</ProtectObjects>")
txtstream~WriteLine("
   <ProtectScenarios>False</ProtectScenarios>")
txtstream~WriteLine("          </WorksheetOptions>")
txtstream~WriteLine("</Worksheet>")
txtstream~WriteLine("</Workbook>")
txtstream~close()
ws~Run(ws~CurrentDirectory || "\ProcessExcel.xml")
```

XSL

The end of the line

BELOW ARE WAYS YOU CAN CREATE XSL FILES TO RENDER YOU XML. Viewer discretion is advised.

```
ws = .OLEObject~new("WScript.Shell")
fso = .OLEObject~new("Scripting.FileSystemObject")
txtstream = fso~OpenTextFile(ws~CurrentDirectory || "\Process.xsl", 2, true, -
2)
```

SINGLE LINE HORIZONTAL

```
txtstream~WriteLine("<?xml version=""1.0" " encoding=""UTF-8" "?>")
txtstream~WriteLine("<xsl:stylesheet                    version=""1.0""
xmlns:xsl=""http://www.w3.org/1999/XSL/Transform" ">")
```

```
txtstream~WriteLine("<xsl:template match="""/"""">")
txtstream~WriteLine("<html>")
txtstream~WriteLine("<head>")
txtstream~WriteLine("<title>Products</title>")
txtstream~WriteLine("<style type='text/css'>")
txtstream~WriteLine("th")
txtstream~WriteLine("{")
txtstream~WriteLine("   COLOR: darkred;")
txtstream~WriteLine("   BACKGROUND-COLOR: white;")
txtstream~WriteLine("   FONT-FAMILY: font-family: Cambria, serif;")
txtstream~WriteLine("   FONT-SIZE: 12px;")
txtstream~WriteLine("   text-align: left;")
txtstream~WriteLine("   white-Space: nowrap;")
txtstream~WriteLine("}")
txtstream~WriteLine("td")
txtstream~WriteLine("{")
txtstream~WriteLine("   COLOR: navy;")
txtstream~WriteLine("   BACKGROUND-COLOR: white;")
txtstream~WriteLine("   FONT-FAMILY: font-family: Cambria, serif;")
txtstream~WriteLine("   FONT-SIZE: 12px;")
txtstream~WriteLine("   text-align: left;")
txtstream~WriteLine("   white-Space: nowrap;")
txtstream~WriteLine("}")
txtstream~WriteLine("</style>")
txtstream~WriteLine("</head>")
txtstream~WriteLine("<body bgcolor=""#333333"" >")
txtstream~WriteLine("<table colspacing=""3"" colpadding=""3"" >")
obj = objs~ItemIndex(0)
txtstream~WriteLine("<tr>")
for Each prop in obj~Properties_
   txtstream~WriteLine("<th>" || prop~Name || </th>")
next
txtstream~WriteLine("</tr>")
```

```
        txtstream~WriteLine("<tr>")
        for Each prop in obj~Properties_
            txtstream~WriteLine("<td><xsl:value-of select=""data/Win32_Process/" ||
prop~Name || """/></td>")
        next
        txtstream~WriteLine("</tr>")
        txtstream~WriteLine("</table>")
        txtstream~WriteLine("</body>")
        txtstream~WriteLine("</html>")
        txtstream~WriteLine("</xsl:template>")
        txtstream~WriteLine("</xsl:stylesheet>")
        txtstream~close()
```

For Multi Line Horizontal

```
        txtstream~WriteLine("<?xml version=""1.0" " encoding=""UTF-8" "?>")
        txtstream~WriteLine("<xsl:stylesheet                           version=""1.0""
xmlns:xsl="""http://www.w3.org/1999/XSL/Transform" ">")
        txtstream~WriteLine("<xsl:template match=""/"">")
        txtstream~WriteLine("<html>")
        txtstream~WriteLine("<head>")
        txtstream~WriteLine("<title>Products</title>")
        txtstream~WriteLine("<style type='text/css'>")
        txtstream~WriteLine("th")
        txtstream~WriteLine("{")
        txtstream~WriteLine("   COLOR: darkred;")
        txtstream~WriteLine("   BACKGROUND-COLOR: white;")
        txtstream~WriteLine("   FONT-FAMILY: font-family: Cambria, serif;")
        txtstream~WriteLine("   FONT-SIZE: 12px;")
        txtstream~WriteLine("   text-align: left;")
        txtstream~WriteLine("   white-Space: nowrap;")
```

```
txtstream~WriteLine("}")
txtstream~WriteLine("td")
txtstream~WriteLine("{")
txtstream~WriteLine("    COLOR: navy;")
txtstream~WriteLine("    BACKGROUND-COLOR: white;")
txtstream~WriteLine("    FONT-FAMILY: font-family: Cambria, serif;")
txtstream~WriteLine("    FONT-SIZE: 12px;")
txtstream~WriteLine("    text-align: left;")
txtstream~WriteLine("    white-Space: nowrap;")
txtstream~WriteLine("}")
txtstream~WriteLine("</style>")
txtstream~WriteLine("</head>")
txtstream~WriteLine("<body bgcolor=""“#333333” "">")
txtstream~WriteLine("<table colspacing=""“3” " colpadding=""“3” "">")


obj = objs~ItemIndex(0)
txtstream~WriteLine("<tr>")
for Each prop in obj~Properties_
   txtstream~WriteLine("<th>" || prop~Name || </th>")
next
txtstream~WriteLine("</tr>")
txtstream~WriteLine("<xsl:for-each select=""”data/Win32_Process”"">")
txtstream~WriteLine("<tr>")
for Each prop in obj~Properties_
   txtstream~WriteLine("<td><xsl:value-of    select=""”    ||    prop~Name    ||
"”"/></td>")
next
txtstream~WriteLine("</tr>")
txtstream~WriteLine("</xsl:for-each>")
txtstream~WriteLine("</table>")
txtstream~WriteLine("</body>")
txtstream~WriteLine("</html>")
```

```
txtstream~WriteLine("</xsl:template>")
txtstream~WriteLine("</xsl:stylesheet>")
txtstream~close()
```

For Single Line Vertical

```
txtstream~WriteLine("<?xml version="“1.0” " encoding="“UTF-8” "?>")
txtstream~WriteLine("<xsl:stylesheet                    version="“1.0”"
xmlns:xsl="“http://www.w3.org/1999/XSL/Transform” ">")
txtstream~WriteLine("<xsl:template match="“/”">“)
txtstream~WriteLine("<html>")
txtstream~WriteLine("<head>")
txtstream~WriteLine("<title>Products</title>")
txtstream~WriteLine("<style type='text/css'>")
txtstream~WriteLine("th")
txtstream~WriteLine("{")
txtstream~WriteLine("   COLOR: darkred;")
txtstream~WriteLine("   BACKGROUND-COLOR: white;")
txtstream~WriteLine("   FONT-FAMILY: font-family: Cambria, serif;")
txtstream~WriteLine("   FONT-SIZE: 12px;")
txtstream~WriteLine("   text-align: left;")
txtstream~WriteLine("   white-Space: nowrap;")
txtstream~WriteLine("}")
txtstream~WriteLine("td")
txtstream~WriteLine("{")
txtstream~WriteLine("   COLOR: navy;")
txtstream~WriteLine("   BACKGROUND-COLOR: white;")
txtstream~WriteLine("   FONT-FAMILY: font-family: Cambria, serif;")
txtstream~WriteLine("   FONT-SIZE: 12px;")
txtstream~WriteLine("   text-align: left;")
txtstream~WriteLine("   white-Space: nowrap;")
txtstream~WriteLine("}")
```

```
txtstream~WriteLine("</style>")
txtstream~WriteLine("</head>")
txtstream~WriteLine("<body bgcolor=""#333333" ">")
txtstream~WriteLine("<table colspacing=""3" " colpadding=""3" ">")

obj = objs.ItemIndex[0]
for Each prop in obj~Properties_
    txtstream~WriteLine("<tr><th>" || prop~Name || </th>")
    txtstream~WriteLine("<td><xsl:value-of select=""data/Win32_Process/" || prop~Name || """/></td></tr>")
next
txtstream~WriteLine("</table>")
txtstream~WriteLine("</body>")
txtstream~WriteLine("</html>")
txtstream~WriteLine("</xsl:template>")
txtstream~WriteLine("</xsl:stylesheet>")
txtstream~close()
```

For Multi Line Vertical

```
txtstream~WriteLine("<?xml version=""1.0" " encoding=""UTF-8" "?>")
txtstream~WriteLine("<xsl:stylesheet                        version=""1.0""
xmlns:xsl=""http://www.w3.org/1999/XSL/Transform" ">")
txtstream~WriteLine("<xsl:template match=""/""">")
txtstream~WriteLine("<html>")
txtstream~WriteLine("<head>")
txtstream~WriteLine("<title>Products</title>")
```

```
txtstream~WriteLine("<style type='text/css'>")
txtstream~WriteLine("th")
txtstream~WriteLine("{")
txtstream~WriteLine("    COLOR: darkred;")
txtstream~WriteLine("    BACKGROUND-COLOR: white;")
txtstream~WriteLine("    FONT-FAMILY: font-family: Cambria, serif;")
txtstream~WriteLine("    FONT-SIZE: 12px;")
txtstream~WriteLine("    text-align: left;")
txtstream~WriteLine("    white-Space: nowrap;")
txtstream~WriteLine("}")
txtstream~WriteLine("td")
txtstream~WriteLine("{")
txtstream~WriteLine("    COLOR: navy;")
txtstream~WriteLine("    BACKGROUND-COLOR: white;")
txtstream~WriteLine("    FONT-FAMILY: font-family: Cambria, serif;")
txtstream~WriteLine("    FONT-SIZE: 12px;")
txtstream~WriteLine("    text-align: left;")
txtstream~WriteLine("    white-Space: nowrap;")
txtstream~WriteLine("}")
txtstream~WriteLine("</style>")
txtstream~WriteLine("</head>")
txtstream~WriteLine("<body bgcolor=""#333333" ">")
txtstream~WriteLine("<table colspacing=""3" " colpadding=""3" ">")

txtstream~WriteLine("<tr>")
obj = objs.ItemIndex[0]
for Each prop in obj~Properties_
    txtstream~WriteLine("<tr><th>" || prop~Name || </th>")
    txtstream~WriteLine("<td><xsl:for-each
select=""data/Win32_Process"">")
        txtstream~WriteLine("<xsl:value-of    select="""    ||    prop~Name    ||
"""/></td>")
    txtstream~WriteLine("</xsl:for-each></tr>")
```

```
next
txtstream~WriteLine("</table>")
txtstream~WriteLine("</body>")
txtstream~WriteLine("</html>")
txtstream~WriteLine("</xsl:template>")
txtstream~WriteLine("</xsl:stylesheet>")
txtstream~close()
```

Stylesheets

The difference between boring and oh, wow!

T HE FIRST PARAGRAPH STYLE GIVES you nice spacing after the title, as well as the right indents for the first part of your text. Try adding uppercase letters to half of the first line for added styling. For even more stylistic impact, add a

Style sheets:

The stylesheets in Appendix A, were used to render these pages. If you find one you like, feel free to use it.

Report:

Table

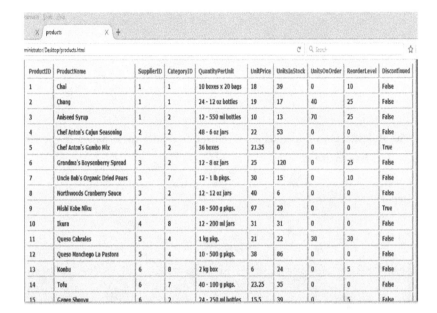

ProductID	ProductName	SupplierID	CategoryID	QuantityPerUnit	UnitPrice	UnitsInStock	UnitsOnOrder	ReorderLevel	Discontinued
1	Chai	1	1	10 boxes x 20 bags	18	39	0	10	False
2	Chang	1	1	24 - 12 oz bottles	19	17	40	25	False
3	Aniseed Syrup	1	2	12 - 550 ml bottles	10	13	70	25	False
4	Chef Anton's Cajun Seasoning	2	2	48 - 6 oz jars	22	53	0	0	False
5	Chef Anton's Gumbo Mix	2	2	36 boxes	21.35	0	0	0	True
6	Grandma's Boysenberry Spread	3	2	12 - 8 oz jars	25	120	0	25	False
7	Uncle Bob's Organic Dried Pears	3	7	12 - 1 lb pkgs.	30	15	0	10	False
8	Northwoods Cranberry Sauce	3	2	12 - 12 oz jars	40	6	0	0	False
9	Mishi Kobe Niku	4	6	18 - 500 g pkgs.	97	29	0	0	True
10	Ikura	4	8	12 - 200 ml jars	31	31	0	0	False
11	Queso Cabrales	5	4	1 kg pkg.	21	22	30	30	False
12	Queso Manchego La Pastora	5	4	10 - 500 g pkgs.	38	86	0	0	False
13	Konbu	6	8	2 kg box	6	24	0	5	False
14	Tofu	6	7	40 - 100 g pkgs.	23.25	35	0	0	False
15	Genen Shouyu	6	2	24 - 250 ml bottles	15.5	39	0	5	False

None:

Black and White

Colored:

AccountExpires	AuthorizationFlags	BadPasswordCount	Caption	CodePage	Comment	CountryCode	Description
			NT AUTHORITY\SYSTEM				Network login profile settings for SYSTEM on NT AUTHORITY
			NT AUTHORITY\LOCAL SERVICE				Network login profile settings for LOCAL SERVICE on NT AUTHORITY
			NT AUTHORITY\NETWORK SERVICE				Network login profile settings for NETWORK SERVICE on NT AUTHORITY
	0	0	Administrator	0	Built-in account for administering the computer/domain	0	Network login profile settings for on WIN-8JRLOAKMF3B
			NT SERVICE\SSASTELEMETRY				Network login profile settings for SSASTELEMETRY on NT SERVICE
			NT SERVICE\SSISTELEMETRY130				Network login profile settings for SSISTELEMETRY130 on NT SERVICE
			NT SERVICE\SQLTELEMETRY				Network login profile settings for SQLTELEMETRY on NT SERVICE
			NT SERVICE\MSSQLServerOLAPService				Network login profile settings for MSSQLServerOLAPService on NT SERVICE
			NT SERVICE\ReportServer				Network login profile settings for ReportServer on NT SERVICE
			NT SERVICE\MSSQLFDLauncher				Network login profile settings for MSSQLFDLauncher on NT SERVICE
			NT SERVICE\MSSQLLaunchpad				Network login profile settings for MSSQLLaunchpad on NT SERVICE
			NT SERVICE\SsrsServer130				Network login profile settings for SsrsServer130 on NT SERVICE
			NT SERVICE\MSSQLSERVER				Network login profile settings for MSSQLSERVER on NT SERVICE
			IIS APPPOOL\Classic .NET AppPool				Network login profile settings for Classic .NET AppPool on IIS APPPOOL
			IIS APPPOOL\.NET v4.5				Network login profile settings for .NET v4.5 on IIS APPPOOL
			IIS APPPOOL\.NET v2.0				Network login profile settings for .NET v2.0 on IIS APPPOOL
			IIS APPPOOL\.NET v4.5 Classic				Network login profile settings for .NET v4.5 Classic on IIS APPPOOL
			IIS APPPOOL\.NET v2.0 Classic				Network login profile settings for .NET v2.0 Classic on IIS APPPOOL

Oscillating:

Availability	BytesPerSector	Capabilities	CapabilityDescriptions	Caption	CompressionMethod	ConfigManagerErrorCode	ConfigManagerUserConfig
	512	3, 4, 10	Random Access, Supports Writing, SMART Notification	OCZ REVODRIVE350 SCSI Disk Device		0	FALSE
	512	3, 4	Random Access, Supports Writing	NVMe TOSHIBA-RD400		0	FALSE
	512	3, 4, 10	Random Access, Supports Writing, SMART Notification	TOSHIBA DT01ACA200		0	FALSE

3D:

Availability	BytesPerSector	Capabilities	CapabilityDescriptions	Caption	CompressionMethod	ConfigManagerErrorCode	ConfigManagerUserConfig	CreationClassName
	512	3, 4, 10	Random Access, Supports Writing, SMART Notification	OCZ REVODRIVE350 SCSI Disk Device		0	FALSE	Win32_DiskDrive
	512	3, 4	Random Access, Supports Writing	NVMe TOSHIBA RD400		0	FALSE	Win32_DiskDrive
	512	3, 4, 10	Random Access, Supports Writing, SMART Notification	TOSHIBA DT01ACA200		0	FALSE	Win32_DiskDrive

Shadow Box:

Availability	BytesPerSector	Capabilities	CapabilityDescriptions	Caption	CompressionMethod	ConfigManagerErrorCode	ConfigManagerUserConfig	CreationClassName	DefaultBlockSize
	512	3, 4, 10	Random Access, Supports Writing, SMART Notification	OCZ REVODRIVE350 SCSI Disk Device		0	FALSE	Win32_DiskDrive	
	512	3, 4	Random Access, Supports Writing	NVMe TOSHIBA RD400		0	FALSE	Win32_DiskDrive	
	512	3, 4, 10	Random Access, Supports Writing, SMART Notification	TOSHIBA DT01ACA200		0	FALSE	Win32_DiskDrive	

Shadow Box Single Line Vertical

BiosCharacteristics	7, 10, 11, 12, 15, 16, 17, 19, 23, 24, 25, 26, 27, 28, 29, 32, 33, 40, 42, 43, 48, 50, 58, 59, 64, 65, 66, 67, 68, 69, 70, 71, 72, 73, 74, 75, 76, 77, 78, 79
BIOSVersion	ALASKA - 1072009, 0504, American Megatrends - 5000C
BuildNumber	
Caption	0504
CodeSet	
CurrentLanguage	en|US|iso8859-1
Description	0504
IdentificationCode	
InstallableLanguages	8
InstallDate	
LanguageEdition	
ListOfLanguages	en|US|iso8859-1, fr|FR|iso8859-1, zh|CN|unicode, , , , ,
Manufacturer	American Megatrends Inc.
Name	0504
OtherTargetOS	
PrimaryBIOS	TRUE

Shadow Box Multi line Vertical

Property	Drive 1	Drive 2	Drive 3
Availability			
BytesPerSector	512	512	512
Capabilities	3, 4, 10	3, 4	3, 4, 10
CapabilityDescriptions	Random Access, Supports Writing, SMART Notification	Random Access, Supports Writing	Random Access, Supports Writing, SMART Notification
Caption	OCZ REVODRIVE350 SCSI Disk Device	NVMe TOSHIBA RD400	TOSHIBA DT01ACA200
CompressionMethod			
ConfigManagerErrorCode	0	0	0
ConfigManagerUserConfig	FALSE	FALSE	FALSE
CreationClassName	Win32_DiskDrive	Win32_DiskDrive	Win32_DiskDrive
DefaultBlockSize			
Description	Disk drive	Disk drive	Disk drive
DeviceID	\\.\PHYSICALDRIVE2	\\.\PHYSICALDRIVE1	\\.\PHYSICALDRIVE0
ErrorCleared			
ErrorDescription			
ErrorMethodology			
FirmwareRevision	2.50	57CT4J05	MX4OABB0
Index	2	1	0

Stylesheets
Decorating your web pages

BELOW ARE SOME STYLESHEETS I COOKED UP THAT I LIKE AND THINK YOU MIGHT TOO. Don't worry I won't be offended if you take and modify to your hearts delight. Please do!

NONE

```
txtstream~WriteLine("<style type='text/css'>")
txtstream~WriteLine("th")
txtstream~WriteLine("{")
txtstream~WriteLine("   COLOR: white;")
txtstream~WriteLine("}")
txtstream~WriteLine("td")
txtstream~WriteLine("{")
txtstream~WriteLine("   COLOR: white;")
txtstream~WriteLine("}")
txtstream~WriteLine("</style>")
```

BLACK AND WHITE TEXT

```
txtstream~WriteLine("<style type='text/css'>")
txtstream~WriteLine("th")
txtstream~WriteLine("{")
txtstream~WriteLine("   COLOR: white;")
txtstream~WriteLine("   BACKGROUND-COLOR: black;")
txtstream~WriteLine("   FONT-FAMILY: font-family: Cambria, serif;")
txtstream~WriteLine("   FONT-SIZE: 12px;")
txtstream~WriteLine("   text-align: left;")
txtstream~WriteLine("   white-Space: nowrap;")
txtstream~WriteLine("}")
txtstream~WriteLine("td")
txtstream~WriteLine("{")
txtstream~WriteLine("   COLOR: white;")
txtstream~WriteLine("   BACKGROUND-COLOR: black;")
txtstream~WriteLine("   FONT-FAMILY: font-family: Cambria, serif;")
txtstream~WriteLine("   FONT-SIZE: 12px;")
txtstream~WriteLine("   text-align: left;")
txtstream~WriteLine("   white-Space: nowrap;")
txtstream~WriteLine("}")
txtstream~WriteLine("div")
txtstream~WriteLine("{")
txtstream~WriteLine("   COLOR: white;")
txtstream~WriteLine("   BACKGROUND-COLOR: black;")
txtstream~WriteLine("   FONT-FAMILY: font-family: Cambria, serif;")
txtstream~WriteLine("   FONT-SIZE: 10px;")
txtstream~WriteLine("   text-align: left;")
txtstream~WriteLine("   white-Space: nowrap;")
txtstream~WriteLine("}")
txtstream~WriteLine("span")
txtstream~WriteLine("{")
txtstream~WriteLine("   COLOR: white;")
txtstream~WriteLine("   BACKGROUND-COLOR: black;")
txtstream~WriteLine("   FONT-FAMILY: font-family: Cambria, serif;")
```

```
txtstream~WriteLine("   FONT-SIZE: 10px;")
txtstream~WriteLine("   text-align: left;")
txtstream~WriteLine("   white-Space: nowrap;")
txtstream~WriteLine("   display:inline-block;")
txtstream~WriteLine("   width: 100%;")
txtstream~WriteLine("}")
txtstream~WriteLine("textarea")
txtstream~WriteLine("{")
txtstream~WriteLine("   COLOR: white;")
txtstream~WriteLine("   BACKGROUND-COLOR: black;")
txtstream~WriteLine("   FONT-FAMILY: font-family: Cambria, serif;")
txtstream~WriteLine("   FONT-SIZE: 10px;")
txtstream~WriteLine("   text-align: left;")
txtstream~WriteLine("   white-Space: nowrap;")
txtstream~WriteLine("   width: 100%;")
txtstream~WriteLine("}")
txtstream~WriteLine("select")
txtstream~WriteLine("{")
txtstream~WriteLine("   COLOR: white;")
txtstream~WriteLine("   BACKGROUND-COLOR: black;")
txtstream~WriteLine("   FONT-FAMILY: font-family: Cambria, serif;")
txtstream~WriteLine("   FONT-SIZE: 10px;")
txtstream~WriteLine("   text-align: left;")
txtstream~WriteLine("   white-Space: nowrap;")
txtstream~WriteLine("   width: 100%;")
txtstream~WriteLine("}")
txtstream~WriteLine("input")
txtstream~WriteLine("{")
txtstream~WriteLine("   COLOR: white;")
txtstream~WriteLine("   BACKGROUND-COLOR: black;")
txtstream~WriteLine("   FONT-FAMILY: font-family: Cambria, serif;")
txtstream~WriteLine("   FONT-SIZE: 12px;")
txtstream~WriteLine("   text-align: left;")
```

```
txtstream~WriteLine("    display:table-cell;")
txtstream~WriteLine("    white-Space: nowrap;")
txtstream~WriteLine("}")
txtstream~WriteLine("h1 {")
txtstream~WriteLine("color: antiquewhite;")
txtstream~WriteLine("text-shadow: 1px 1px 1px black;")
txtstream~WriteLine("padding: 3px;")
txtstream~WriteLine("text-align: center;")
txtstream~WriteLine("box-shadow: inset 2px 2px 5px rgba(0,0,0,0.5), inset -2px -2px 5px rgba(255,255,255,0.5);")
txtstream~WriteLine("}")
txtstream~WriteLine("</style>")
```

COLORED TEXT

```
txtstream~WriteLine("<style type='text/css'>")
txtstream~WriteLine("th")
txtstream~WriteLine("{")
txtstream~WriteLine("    COLOR: darkred;")
txtstream~WriteLine("    BACKGROUND-COLOR: #eeeeee;")
txtstream~WriteLine("    FONT-FAMILY: font-family: Cambria, serif;")
txtstream~WriteLine("    FONT-SIZE: 12px;")
txtstream~WriteLine("    text-align: left;")
txtstream~WriteLine("    white-Space: nowrap;")
txtstream~WriteLine("}")
txtstream~WriteLine("td")
txtstream~WriteLine("{")
txtstream~WriteLine("    COLOR: navy;")
txtstream~WriteLine("    BACKGROUND-COLOR: #eeeeee;")
txtstream~WriteLine("    FONT-FAMILY: font-family: Cambria, serif;")
txtstream~WriteLine("    FONT-SIZE: 12px;")
txtstream~WriteLine("    text-align: left;")
txtstream~WriteLine("    white-Space: nowrap;")
```

```
txtstream~WriteLine("}")
txtstream~WriteLine("div")
txtstream~WriteLine("{")
txtstream~WriteLine("    COLOR: white;")
txtstream~WriteLine("    BACKGROUND-COLOR: navy;")
txtstream~WriteLine("    FONT-FAMILY: font-family: Cambria, serif;")
txtstream~WriteLine("    FONT-SIZE: 10px;")
txtstream~WriteLine("    text-align: left;")
txtstream~WriteLine("    white-Space: nowrap;")
txtstream~WriteLine("}")
txtstream~WriteLine("span")
txtstream~WriteLine("{")
txtstream~WriteLine("    COLOR: white;")
txtstream~WriteLine("    BACKGROUND-COLOR: navy;")
txtstream~WriteLine("    FONT-FAMILY: font-family: Cambria, serif;")
txtstream~WriteLine("    FONT-SIZE: 10px;")
txtstream~WriteLine("    text-align: left;")
txtstream~WriteLine("    white-Space: nowrap;")
txtstream~WriteLine("    display:inline-block;")
txtstream~WriteLine("    width: 100%;")
txtstream~WriteLine("}")
txtstream~WriteLine("textarea")
txtstream~WriteLine("{")
txtstream~WriteLine("    COLOR: white;")
txtstream~WriteLine("    BACKGROUND-COLOR: navy;")
txtstream~WriteLine("    FONT-FAMILY: font-family: Cambria, serif;")
txtstream~WriteLine("    FONT-SIZE: 10px;")
txtstream~WriteLine("    text-align: left;")
txtstream~WriteLine("    white-Space: nowrap;")
txtstream~WriteLine("    width: 100%;")
txtstream~WriteLine("}")
txtstream~WriteLine("select")
txtstream~WriteLine("{")
```

```
txtstream~WriteLine("    COLOR: white;")
txtstream~WriteLine("    BACKGROUND-COLOR: navy;")
txtstream~WriteLine("    FONT-FAMILY: font-family: Cambria, serif;")
txtstream~WriteLine("    FONT-SIZE: 10px;")
txtstream~WriteLine("    text-align: left;")
txtstream~WriteLine("    white-Space: nowrap;")
txtstream~WriteLine("    width: 100%;")
txtstream~WriteLine("}")
txtstream~WriteLine("input")
txtstream~WriteLine("{")
txtstream~WriteLine("    COLOR: white;")
txtstream~WriteLine("    BACKGROUND-COLOR: navy;")
txtstream~WriteLine("    FONT-FAMILY: font-family: Cambria, serif;")
txtstream~WriteLine("    FONT-SIZE: 12px;")
txtstream~WriteLine("    text-align: left;")
txtstream~WriteLine("    display:table-cell;")
txtstream~WriteLine("    white-Space: nowrap;")
txtstream~WriteLine("}")
txtstream~WriteLine("h1 {")
txtstream~WriteLine("color: antiquewhite;")
txtstream~WriteLine("text-shadow: 1px 1px 1px black;")
txtstream~WriteLine("padding: 3px;")
txtstream~WriteLine("text-align: center;")
txtstream~WriteLine("box-shadow: inset 2px 2px 5px rgba(0,0,0,0.5), inset -2px -2px 5px rgba(255,255,255,0.5);")
txtstream~WriteLine("}")
txtstream~WriteLine("</style>")
```

OSCILLATING ROW COLORS

```
txtstream~WriteLine("<style>")
```

```
txtstream~WriteLine("th")
txtstream~WriteLine("{")
txtstream~WriteLine("    COLOR: white;")
txtstream~WriteLine("    BACKGROUND-COLOR: navy;")
txtstream~WriteLine("    FONT-FAMILY: font-family: Cambria, serif;")
txtstream~WriteLine("    FONT-SIZE: 12px;")
txtstream~WriteLine("    text-align: left;")
txtstream~WriteLine("    white-Space: nowrap;")
txtstream~WriteLine("}")
txtstream~WriteLine("td")
txtstream~WriteLine("{")
txtstream~WriteLine("    COLOR: navy;")
txtstream~WriteLine("    FONT-FAMILY: font-family: Cambria, serif;")
txtstream~WriteLine("    FONT-SIZE: 12px;")
txtstream~WriteLine("    text-align: left;")
txtstream~WriteLine("    white-Space: nowrap;")
txtstream~WriteLine("}")
txtstream~WriteLine("div")
txtstream~WriteLine("{")
txtstream~WriteLine("    COLOR: navy;")
txtstream~WriteLine("    FONT-FAMILY: font-family: Cambria, serif;")
txtstream~WriteLine("    FONT-SIZE: 12px;")
txtstream~WriteLine("    text-align: left;")
txtstream~WriteLine("    white-Space: nowrap;")
txtstream~WriteLine("}")
txtstream~WriteLine("span")
txtstream~WriteLine("{")
txtstream~WriteLine("    COLOR: navy;")
txtstream~WriteLine("    FONT-FAMILY: font-family: Cambria, serif;")
txtstream~WriteLine("    FONT-SIZE: 12px;")
txtstream~WriteLine("    text-align: left;")
txtstream~WriteLine("    white-Space: nowrap;")
txtstream~WriteLine("    width: 100%;")
```

```
txtstream~WriteLine("}")
txtstream~WriteLine("textarea")
txtstream~WriteLine("{")
txtstream~WriteLine("   COLOR: navy;")
txtstream~WriteLine("   FONT-FAMILY: font-family: Cambria, serif;")
txtstream~WriteLine("   FONT-SIZE: 12px;")
txtstream~WriteLine("   text-align: left;")
txtstream~WriteLine("   white-Space: nowrap;")
txtstream~WriteLine("   display:inline-block;")
txtstream~WriteLine("   width: 100%;")
txtstream~WriteLine("}")
txtstream~WriteLine("select")
txtstream~WriteLine("{")
txtstream~WriteLine("   COLOR: navy;")
txtstream~WriteLine("   FONT-FAMILY: font-family: Cambria, serif;")
txtstream~WriteLine("   FONT-SIZE: 10px;")
txtstream~WriteLine("   text-align: left;")
txtstream~WriteLine("   white-Space: nowrap;")
txtstream~WriteLine("   display:inline-block;")
txtstream~WriteLine("   width: 100%;")
txtstream~WriteLine("}")
txtstream~WriteLine("input")
txtstream~WriteLine("{")
txtstream~WriteLine("   COLOR: navy;")
txtstream~WriteLine("   FONT-FAMILY: font-family: Cambria, serif;")
txtstream~WriteLine("   FONT-SIZE: 12px;")
txtstream~WriteLine("   text-align: left;")
txtstream~WriteLine("   display:table-cell;")
txtstream~WriteLine("   white-Space: nowrap;")
txtstream~WriteLine("}")
txtstream~WriteLine("h1 {")
txtstream~WriteLine("color: antiquewhite;")
txtstream~WriteLine("text-shadow: 1px 1px 1px black;")
```

```
txtstream~WriteLine("padding: 3px;")
txtstream~WriteLine("text-align: center;")
txtstream~WriteLine("box-shadow: inset 2px 2px 5px rgba(0,0,0,0.5), inset -
2px -2px 5px rgba(255,255,255,0.5);")
txtstream~WriteLine("}")
txtstream~WriteLine("tr:nth-child(even){background-color:#f2f2f2;}")
txtstream~WriteLine("tr:nth-child(odd){background-color:#cccccc;
color:#f2f2f2;}")
txtstream~WriteLine("</style>")
```

GHOST DECORATED

```
txtstream~WriteLine("<style type='text/css'>")
txtstream~WriteLine("th")
txtstream~WriteLine("{")
txtstream~WriteLine("   COLOR: black;")
txtstream~WriteLine("   BACKGROUND-COLOR: white;")
txtstream~WriteLine("   FONT-FAMILY: font-family: Cambria, serif;")
txtstream~WriteLine("   FONT-SIZE: 12px;")
txtstream~WriteLine("   text-align: left;")
txtstream~WriteLine("   white-Space: nowrap;")
txtstream~WriteLine("}")
txtstream~WriteLine("td")
txtstream~WriteLine("{")
txtstream~WriteLine("   COLOR: black;")
txtstream~WriteLine("   BACKGROUND-COLOR: white;")
txtstream~WriteLine("   FONT-FAMILY: font-family: Cambria, serif;")
txtstream~WriteLine("   FONT-SIZE: 12px;")
txtstream~WriteLine("   text-align: left;")
txtstream~WriteLine("   white-Space: nowrap;")
txtstream~WriteLine("}")
txtstream~WriteLine("div")
txtstream~WriteLine("{")
```

```
txtstream~WriteLine("    COLOR: black;")
txtstream~WriteLine("    BACKGROUND-COLOR: white;")
txtstream~WriteLine("    FONT-FAMILY: font-family: Cambria, serif;")
txtstream~WriteLine("    FONT-SIZE: 10px;")
txtstream~WriteLine("    text-align: left;")
txtstream~WriteLine("    white-Space: nowrap;")
txtstream~WriteLine("}")
txtstream~WriteLine("span")
txtstream~WriteLine("{")
txtstream~WriteLine("    COLOR: black;")
txtstream~WriteLine("    BACKGROUND-COLOR: white;")
txtstream~WriteLine("    FONT-FAMILY: font-family: Cambria, serif;")
txtstream~WriteLine("    FONT-SIZE: 10px;")
txtstream~WriteLine("    text-align: left;")
txtstream~WriteLine("    white-Space: nowrap;")
txtstream~WriteLine("    display:inline-block;")
txtstream~WriteLine("    width: 100%;")
txtstream~WriteLine("}")
txtstream~WriteLine("textarea")
txtstream~WriteLine("{")
txtstream~WriteLine("    COLOR: black;")
txtstream~WriteLine("    BACKGROUND-COLOR: white;")
txtstream~WriteLine("    FONT-FAMILY: font-family: Cambria, serif;")
txtstream~WriteLine("    FONT-SIZE: 10px;")
txtstream~WriteLine("    text-align: left;")
txtstream~WriteLine("    white-Space: nowrap;")
txtstream~WriteLine("    width: 100%;")
txtstream~WriteLine("}")
txtstream~WriteLine("select")
txtstream~WriteLine("{")
txtstream~WriteLine("    COLOR: black;")
txtstream~WriteLine("    BACKGROUND-COLOR: white;")
txtstream~WriteLine("    FONT-FAMILY: font-family: Cambria, serif;")
```

```
txtstream~WriteLine("    FONT-SIZE: 10px;")
txtstream~WriteLine("    text-align: left;")
txtstream~WriteLine("    white-Space: nowrap;")
txtstream~WriteLine("    width: 100%;")
txtstream~WriteLine("}")
txtstream~WriteLine("input")
txtstream~WriteLine("{")
txtstream~WriteLine("    COLOR: black;")
txtstream~WriteLine("    BACKGROUND-COLOR: white;")
txtstream~WriteLine("    FONT-FAMILY: font-family: Cambria, serif;")
txtstream~WriteLine("    FONT-SIZE: 12px;")
txtstream~WriteLine("    text-align: left;")
txtstream~WriteLine("    display:table-cell;")
txtstream~WriteLine("    white-Space: nowrap;")
txtstream~WriteLine("}")
txtstream~WriteLine("h1 {")
txtstream~WriteLine("color: antiquewhite;")
txtstream~WriteLine("text-shadow: 1px 1px 1px black;")
txtstream~WriteLine("padding: 3px;")
txtstream~WriteLine("text-align: center;")
txtstream~WriteLine("box-shadow: inset 2px 2px 5px rgba(0,0,0,0.5), inset -
2px -2px 5px rgba(255,255,255,0.5);")
txtstream~WriteLine("}")
txtstream~WriteLine("</style>")
```

3D

```
txtstream~WriteLine("<style type='text/css'>")
txtstream~WriteLine("body")
txtstream~WriteLine("{")
txtstream~WriteLine("    PADDING-RIGHT: 0px;")
txtstream~WriteLine("    PADDING-LEFT: 0px;")
```

```
txtstream~WriteLine("    PADDING-BOTTOM: 0px;")
txtstream~WriteLine("    MARGIN: 0px;")
txtstream~WriteLine("    COLOR: #333;")
txtstream~WriteLine("    PADDING-TOP: 0px;")
txtstream~WriteLine("    FONT-FAMILY: verdana, arial, helvetica, sans-serif;")
txtstream~WriteLine("}")
txtstream~WriteLine("table")
txtstream~WriteLine("{")
txtstream~WriteLine("    BORDER-RIGHT: #999999 3px solid;")
txtstream~WriteLine("    PADDING-RIGHT: 6px;")
txtstream~WriteLine("    PADDING-LEFT: 6px;")
txtstream~WriteLine("    FONT-WEIGHT: Bold;")
txtstream~WriteLine("    FONT-SIZE: 14px;")
txtstream~WriteLine("    PADDING-BOTTOM: 6px;")
txtstream~WriteLine("    COLOR: Peru;")
txtstream~WriteLine("    LINE-HEIGHT: 14px;")
txtstream~WriteLine("    PADDING-TOP: 6px;")
txtstream~WriteLine("    BORDER-BOTTOM: #999 1px solid;")
txtstream~WriteLine("    BACKGROUND-COLOR: #eeeeee;")
txtstream~WriteLine("    FONT-FAMILY: verdana, arial, helvetica, sans-serif;")
txtstream~WriteLine("    FONT-SIZE: 12px;")
txtstream~WriteLine("}")
txtstream~WriteLine("th")
txtstream~WriteLine("{")
txtstream~WriteLine("    BORDER-RIGHT: #999999 3px solid;")
txtstream~WriteLine("    PADDING-RIGHT: 6px;")
txtstream~WriteLine("    PADDING-LEFT: 6px;")
txtstream~WriteLine("    FONT-WEIGHT: Bold;")
txtstream~WriteLine("    FONT-SIZE: 14px;")
txtstream~WriteLine("    PADDING-BOTTOM: 6px;")
txtstream~WriteLine("    COLOR: darkred;")
txtstream~WriteLine("    LINE-HEIGHT: 14px;")
txtstream~WriteLine("    PADDING-TOP: 6px;")
```

```
txtstream~WriteLine("   BORDER-BOTTOM: #999 1px solid;")
txtstream~WriteLine("   BACKGROUND-COLOR: #eeeeee;")
txtstream~WriteLine("   FONT-FAMILY: font-family: Cambria, serif;")
txtstream~WriteLine("   FONT-SIZE: 12px;")
txtstream~WriteLine("   text-align: left;")
txtstream~WriteLine("   white-Space: nowrap;")
txtstream~WriteLine("}")
txtstream~WriteLine(".th")
txtstream~WriteLine("{")
txtstream~WriteLine("   BORDER-RIGHT: #999999 2px solid;")
txtstream~WriteLine("   PADDING-RIGHT: 6px;")
txtstream~WriteLine("   PADDING-LEFT: 6px;")
txtstream~WriteLine("   FONT-WEIGHT: Bold;")
txtstream~WriteLine("   PADDING-BOTTOM: 6px;")
txtstream~WriteLine("   COLOR: black;")
txtstream~WriteLine("   PADDING-TOP: 6px;")
txtstream~WriteLine("   BORDER-BOTTOM: #999 2px solid;")
txtstream~WriteLine("   BACKGROUND-COLOR: #eeeeee;")
txtstream~WriteLine("   FONT-FAMILY: font-family: Cambria, serif;")
txtstream~WriteLine("   FONT-SIZE: 10px;")
txtstream~WriteLine("   text-align: right;")
txtstream~WriteLine("   white-Space: nowrap;")
txtstream~WriteLine("}")
txtstream~WriteLine("td")
txtstream~WriteLine("{")
txtstream~WriteLine("   BORDER-RIGHT: #999999 3px solid;")
txtstream~WriteLine("   PADDING-RIGHT: 6px;")
txtstream~WriteLine("   PADDING-LEFT: 6px;")
txtstream~WriteLine("   FONT-WEIGHT: Normal;")
txtstream~WriteLine("   PADDING-BOTTOM: 6px;")
txtstream~WriteLine("   COLOR: navy;")
txtstream~WriteLine("   LINE-HEIGHT: 14px;")
txtstream~WriteLine("   PADDING-TOP: 6px;")
```

```
txtstream~WriteLine("    BORDER-BOTTOM: #999 1px solid;")
txtstream~WriteLine("    BACKGROUND-COLOR: #eeeeee;")
txtstream~WriteLine("    FONT-FAMILY: font-family: Cambria, serif;")
txtstream~WriteLine("    FONT-SIZE: 12px;")
txtstream~WriteLine("    text-align: left;")
txtstream~WriteLine("    white-Space: nowrap;")
txtstream~WriteLine("}")
txtstream~WriteLine("div")
txtstream~WriteLine("{")
txtstream~WriteLine("    BORDER-RIGHT: #999999 3px solid;")
txtstream~WriteLine("    PADDING-RIGHT: 6px;")
txtstream~WriteLine("    PADDING-LEFT: 6px;")
txtstream~WriteLine("    FONT-WEIGHT: Normal;")
txtstream~WriteLine("    PADDING-BOTTOM: 6px;")
txtstream~WriteLine("    COLOR: white;")
txtstream~WriteLine("    PADDING-TOP: 6px;")
txtstream~WriteLine("    BORDER-BOTTOM: #999 1px solid;")
txtstream~WriteLine("    BACKGROUND-COLOR: navy;")
txtstream~WriteLine("    FONT-FAMILY: font-family: Cambria, serif;")
txtstream~WriteLine("    FONT-SIZE: 10px;")
txtstream~WriteLine("    text-align: left;")
txtstream~WriteLine("    white-Space: nowrap;")
txtstream~WriteLine("}")
txtstream~WriteLine("span")
txtstream~WriteLine("{")
txtstream~WriteLine("    BORDER-RIGHT: #999999 3px solid;")
txtstream~WriteLine("    PADDING-RIGHT: 3px;")
txtstream~WriteLine("    PADDING-LEFT: 3px;")
txtstream~WriteLine("    FONT-WEIGHT: Normal;")
txtstream~WriteLine("    PADDING-BOTTOM: 3px;")
txtstream~WriteLine("    COLOR: white;")
txtstream~WriteLine("    PADDING-TOP: 3px;")
txtstream~WriteLine("    BORDER-BOTTOM: #999 1px solid;")
```

```
txtstream~WriteLine("    BACKGROUND-COLOR: navy;")
txtstream~WriteLine("    FONT-FAMILY: font-family: Cambria, serif;")
txtstream~WriteLine("    FONT-SIZE: 10px;")
txtstream~WriteLine("    text-align: left;")
txtstream~WriteLine("    white-Space: nowrap;")
txtstream~WriteLine("    display:inline-block;")
txtstream~WriteLine("    width: 100%;")
txtstream~WriteLine("}")
txtstream~WriteLine("textarea")
txtstream~WriteLine("{")
txtstream~WriteLine("    BORDER-RIGHT: #999999 3px solid;")
txtstream~WriteLine("    PADDING-RIGHT: 3px;")
txtstream~WriteLine("    PADDING-LEFT: 3px;")
txtstream~WriteLine("    FONT-WEIGHT: Normal;")
txtstream~WriteLine("    PADDING-BOTTOM: 3px;")
txtstream~WriteLine("    COLOR: white;")
txtstream~WriteLine("    PADDING-TOP: 3px;")
txtstream~WriteLine("    BORDER-BOTTOM: #999 1px solid;")
txtstream~WriteLine("    BACKGROUND-COLOR: navy;")
txtstream~WriteLine("    FONT-FAMILY: font-family: Cambria, serif;")
txtstream~WriteLine("    FONT-SIZE: 10px;")
txtstream~WriteLine("    text-align: left;")
txtstream~WriteLine("    white-Space: nowrap;")
txtstream~WriteLine("    width: 100%;")
txtstream~WriteLine("}")
txtstream~WriteLine("select")
txtstream~WriteLine("{")
txtstream~WriteLine("    BORDER-RIGHT: #999999 3px solid;")
txtstream~WriteLine("    PADDING-RIGHT: 6px;")
txtstream~WriteLine("    PADDING-LEFT: 6px;")
txtstream~WriteLine("    FONT-WEIGHT: Normal;")
txtstream~WriteLine("    PADDING-BOTTOM: 6px;")
txtstream~WriteLine("    COLOR: white;")
```

```
txtstream~WriteLine("    PADDING-TOP: 6px;")
txtstream~WriteLine("    BORDER-BOTTOM: #999 1px solid;")
txtstream~WriteLine("    BACKGROUND-COLOR: navy;")
txtstream~WriteLine("    FONT-FAMILY: font-family: Cambria, serif;")
txtstream~WriteLine("    FONT-SIZE: 10px;")
txtstream~WriteLine("    text-align: left;")
txtstream~WriteLine("    white-Space: nowrap;")
txtstream~WriteLine("    width: 100%;")
txtstream~WriteLine("}")
txtstream~WriteLine("input")
txtstream~WriteLine("{")
txtstream~WriteLine("    BORDER-RIGHT: #999999 3px solid;")
txtstream~WriteLine("    PADDING-RIGHT: 3px;")
txtstream~WriteLine("    PADDING-LEFT: 3px;")
txtstream~WriteLine("    FONT-WEIGHT: Bold;")
txtstream~WriteLine("    PADDING-BOTTOM: 3px;")
txtstream~WriteLine("    COLOR: white;")
txtstream~WriteLine("    PADDING-TOP: 3px;")
txtstream~WriteLine("    BORDER-BOTTOM: #999 1px solid;")
txtstream~WriteLine("    BACKGROUND-COLOR: navy;")
txtstream~WriteLine("    FONT-FAMILY: font-family: Cambria, serif;")
txtstream~WriteLine("    FONT-SIZE: 12px;")
txtstream~WriteLine("    text-align: left;")
txtstream~WriteLine("    display:table-cell;")
txtstream~WriteLine("    white-Space: nowrap;")
txtstream~WriteLine("    width: 100%;")
txtstream~WriteLine("}")
txtstream~WriteLine("h1 {")
txtstream~WriteLine("color: antiquewhite;")
txtstream~WriteLine("text-shadow: 1px 1px 1px black;")
txtstream~WriteLine("padding: 3px;")
txtstream~WriteLine("text-align: center;")
```

```
txtstream~WriteLine("box-shadow: inset 2px 2px 5px rgba(0,0,0,0.5), inset -
2px -2px 5px rgba(255,255,255,0.5);")
txtstream~WriteLine("}")
txtstream~WriteLine("</style>")
```

SHADOW BOX

```
txtstream~WriteLine("<style type='text/css'>")
txtstream~WriteLine("body")
txtstream~WriteLine("{")
txtstream~WriteLine("    PADDING-RIGHT: 0px;")
txtstream~WriteLine("    PADDING-LEFT: 0px;")
txtstream~WriteLine("    PADDING-BOTTOM: 0px;")
txtstream~WriteLine("    MARGIN: 0px;")
txtstream~WriteLine("    COLOR: #333;")
txtstream~WriteLine("    PADDING-TOP: 0px;")
txtstream~WriteLine("    FONT-FAMILY: verdana, arial, helvetica, sans-serif;")
txtstream~WriteLine("}")
txtstream~WriteLine("table")
txtstream~WriteLine("{")
txtstream~WriteLine("    BORDER-RIGHT: #999999 1px solid;")
txtstream~WriteLine("    PADDING-RIGHT: 1px;")
txtstream~WriteLine("    PADDING-LEFT: 1px;")
txtstream~WriteLine("    PADDING-BOTTOM: 1px;")
txtstream~WriteLine("    LINE-HEIGHT: 8px;")
txtstream~WriteLine("    PADDING-TOP: 1px;")
txtstream~WriteLine("    BORDER-BOTTOM: #999 1px solid;")
txtstream~WriteLine("    BACKGROUND-COLOR: #eeeeee;")
txtstream~WriteLine("
filter:progid:DXImageTransform.Microsoft.Shadow(color='silver',    Direction=135,
Strength=16)")
txtstream~WriteLine("}")
txtstream~WriteLine("th")
```

```
txtstream~WriteLine("{")
txtstream~WriteLine("    BORDER-RIGHT: #999999 3px solid;")
txtstream~WriteLine("    PADDING-RIGHT: 6px;")
txtstream~WriteLine("    PADDING-LEFT: 6px;")
txtstream~WriteLine("    FONT-WEIGHT: Bold;")
txtstream~WriteLine("    FONT-SIZE: 14px;")
txtstream~WriteLine("    PADDING-BOTTOM: 6px;")
txtstream~WriteLine("    COLOR: darkred;")
txtstream~WriteLine("    LINE-HEIGHT: 14px;")
txtstream~WriteLine("    PADDING-TOP: 6px;")
txtstream~WriteLine("    BORDER-BOTTOM: #999 1px solid;")
txtstream~WriteLine("    BACKGROUND-COLOR: #eeeeee;")
txtstream~WriteLine("    FONT-FAMILY: font-family: Cambria, serif;")
txtstream~WriteLine("    FONT-SIZE: 12px;")
txtstream~WriteLine("    text-align: left;")
txtstream~WriteLine("    white-Space: nowrap;")
txtstream~WriteLine("}")
txtstream~WriteLine(".th")
txtstream~WriteLine("{")
txtstream~WriteLine("    BORDER-RIGHT: #999999 2px solid;")
txtstream~WriteLine("    PADDING-RIGHT: 6px;")
txtstream~WriteLine("    PADDING-LEFT: 6px;")
txtstream~WriteLine("    FONT-WEIGHT: Bold;")
txtstream~WriteLine("    PADDING-BOTTOM: 6px;")
txtstream~WriteLine("    COLOR: black;")
txtstream~WriteLine("    PADDING-TOP: 6px;")
txtstream~WriteLine("    BORDER-BOTTOM: #999 2px solid;")
txtstream~WriteLine("    BACKGROUND-COLOR: #eeeeee;")
txtstream~WriteLine("    FONT-FAMILY: font-family: Cambria, serif;")
txtstream~WriteLine("    FONT-SIZE: 10px;")
txtstream~WriteLine("    text-align: right;")
txtstream~WriteLine("    white-Space: nowrap;")
txtstream~WriteLine("}")
```

```
txtstream~WriteLine("td")
txtstream~WriteLine("{")
txtstream~WriteLine("    BORDER-RIGHT: #999999 3px solid;")
txtstream~WriteLine("    PADDING-RIGHT: 6px;")
txtstream~WriteLine("    PADDING-LEFT: 6px;")
txtstream~WriteLine("    FONT-WEIGHT: Normal;")
txtstream~WriteLine("    PADDING-BOTTOM: 6px;")
txtstream~WriteLine("    COLOR: navy;")
txtstream~WriteLine("    LINE-HEIGHT: 14px;")
txtstream~WriteLine("    PADDING-TOP: 6px;")
txtstream~WriteLine("    BORDER-BOTTOM: #999 1px solid;")
txtstream~WriteLine("    BACKGROUND-COLOR: #eeeeee;")
txtstream~WriteLine("    FONT-FAMILY: font-family: Cambria, serif;")
txtstream~WriteLine("    FONT-SIZE: 12px;")
txtstream~WriteLine("    text-align: left;")
txtstream~WriteLine("    white-Space: nowrap;")
txtstream~WriteLine("}")
txtstream~WriteLine("div")
txtstream~WriteLine("{")
txtstream~WriteLine("    BORDER-RIGHT: #999999 3px solid;")
txtstream~WriteLine("    PADDING-RIGHT: 6px;")
txtstream~WriteLine("    PADDING-LEFT: 6px;")
txtstream~WriteLine("    FONT-WEIGHT: Normal;")
txtstream~WriteLine("    PADDING-BOTTOM: 6px;")
txtstream~WriteLine("    COLOR: white;")
txtstream~WriteLine("    PADDING-TOP: 6px;")
txtstream~WriteLine("    BORDER-BOTTOM: #999 1px solid;")
txtstream~WriteLine("    BACKGROUND-COLOR: navy;")
txtstream~WriteLine("    FONT-FAMILY: font-family: Cambria, serif;")
txtstream~WriteLine("    FONT-SIZE: 10px;")
txtstream~WriteLine("    text-align: left;")
txtstream~WriteLine("    white-Space: nowrap;")
txtstream~WriteLine("}")
```

```
txtstream~WriteLine("span")
txtstream~WriteLine("{")
txtstream~WriteLine("   BORDER-RIGHT: #999999 3px solid;")
txtstream~WriteLine("   PADDING-RIGHT: 3px;")
txtstream~WriteLine("   PADDING-LEFT: 3px;")
txtstream~WriteLine("   FONT-WEIGHT: Normal;")
txtstream~WriteLine("   PADDING-BOTTOM: 3px;")
txtstream~WriteLine("   COLOR: white;")
txtstream~WriteLine("   PADDING-TOP: 3px;")
txtstream~WriteLine("   BORDER-BOTTOM: #999 1px solid;")
txtstream~WriteLine("   BACKGROUND-COLOR: navy;")
txtstream~WriteLine("   FONT-FAMILY: font-family: Cambria, serif;")
txtstream~WriteLine("   FONT-SIZE: 10px;")
txtstream~WriteLine("   text-align: left;")
txtstream~WriteLine("   white-Space: nowrap;")
txtstream~WriteLine("   display: inline-block;")
txtstream~WriteLine("   width: 100%;")
txtstream~WriteLine("}")
txtstream~WriteLine("textarea")
txtstream~WriteLine("{")
txtstream~WriteLine("   BORDER-RIGHT: #999999 3px solid;")
txtstream~WriteLine("   PADDING-RIGHT: 3px;")
txtstream~WriteLine("   PADDING-LEFT: 3px;")
txtstream~WriteLine("   FONT-WEIGHT: Normal;")
txtstream~WriteLine("   PADDING-BOTTOM: 3px;")
txtstream~WriteLine("   COLOR: white;")
txtstream~WriteLine("   PADDING-TOP: 3px;")
txtstream~WriteLine("   BORDER-BOTTOM: #999 1px solid;")
txtstream~WriteLine("   BACKGROUND-COLOR: navy;")
txtstream~WriteLine("   FONT-FAMILY: font-family: Cambria, serif;")
txtstream~WriteLine("   FONT-SIZE: 10px;")
txtstream~WriteLine("   text-align: left;")
txtstream~WriteLine("   white-Space: nowrap;")
```

```
txtstream~WriteLine("    width: 100%;")
txtstream~WriteLine("}")
txtstream~WriteLine("select")
txtstream~WriteLine("{")
txtstream~WriteLine("    BORDER-RIGHT: #999999 3px solid;")
txtstream~WriteLine("    PADDING-RIGHT: 6px;")
txtstream~WriteLine("    PADDING-LEFT: 6px;")
txtstream~WriteLine("    FONT-WEIGHT: Normal;")
txtstream~WriteLine("    PADDING-BOTTOM: 6px;")
txtstream~WriteLine("    COLOR: white;")
txtstream~WriteLine("    PADDING-TOP: 6px;")
txtstream~WriteLine("    BORDER-BOTTOM: #999 1px solid;")
txtstream~WriteLine("    BACKGROUND-COLOR: navy;")
txtstream~WriteLine("    FONT-FAMILY: font-family: Cambria, serif;")
txtstream~WriteLine("    FONT-SIZE: 10px;")
txtstream~WriteLine("    text-align: left;")
txtstream~WriteLine("    white-Space: nowrap;")
txtstream~WriteLine("    width: 100%;")
txtstream~WriteLine("}")
txtstream~WriteLine("input")
txtstream~WriteLine("{")
txtstream~WriteLine("    BORDER-RIGHT: #999999 3px solid;")
txtstream~WriteLine("    PADDING-RIGHT: 3px;")
txtstream~WriteLine("    PADDING-LEFT: 3px;")
txtstream~WriteLine("    FONT-WEIGHT: Bold;")
txtstream~WriteLine("    PADDING-BOTTOM: 3px;")
txtstream~WriteLine("    COLOR: white;")
txtstream~WriteLine("    PADDING-TOP: 3px;")
txtstream~WriteLine("    BORDER-BOTTOM: #999 1px solid;")
txtstream~WriteLine("    BACKGROUND-COLOR: navy;")
txtstream~WriteLine("    FONT-FAMILY: font-family: Cambria, serif;")
txtstream~WriteLine("    FONT-SIZE: 12px;")
txtstream~WriteLine("    text-align: left;")
```

```
txtstream~WriteLine("    display: table-cell;")
txtstream~WriteLine("    white-Space: nowrap;")
txtstream~WriteLine("    width: 100%;")
txtstream~WriteLine("}")
txtstream~WriteLine("h1 {")
txtstream~WriteLine("color: antiquewhite;")
txtstream~WriteLine("text-shadow: 1px 1px 1px black;")
txtstream~WriteLine("padding: 3px;")
txtstream~WriteLine("text-align: center;")
txtstream~WriteLine("box-shadow: inset 2px 2px 5px rgba(0,0,0,0.5), inset -2px -2px 5px rgba(255,255,255,0.5);")
txtstream~WriteLine("}")
txtstream~WriteLine("</style>")
```

www.ingramcontent.com/pod-product-compliance
Lightning Source LLC
Chambersburg PA
CBHW070847070326
40690CB00009B/1727